Cultivating Connections

Building Supportive Cultural Environments in an Age Marked by Loneliness, Alienation, and Distrust

JUDD ALLEN, Ph.D.

Copyright ©2025 by Judd Allen. All rights reserved. No part of this publication may be reproduced, distributed, or transmitted in any form or by any means, including photocopying, recording, or other electronic or mechanical methods, without the prior written permission of the publisher, except in the case of brief quotations embodied in critical reviews and certain other noncommercial uses permitted by copyright law. For permission requests, write to the publisher at: Human Resources Institute, LLC, www.healthyculture.com, 151 Dunder Road, Burlington, Vermont 05401 USA, JuddA@healthyculture.com (802) 862-8855. Ordering Information: Special discounts are available for quantity purchases by organizations, associations, and other groups. For details, contact the publisher. Library of Congress Cataloging-in-Publication Data Names: Allen, Judd, 1958 - author. Cultivating Connections: Building Supportive Cultural Environments in an Age Marked by Loneliness, Alienation, and Distrust. Description: Burlington, Vermont: HealthyCulture.com [2025] Includes bibliographical references. Identifiers: eBook ISBN 978-0-941703-55-0; paperback ISBN 978-0-941703-53-6 Hardcover/Cloth ISBN 978-0-941703-54-3

Subjects:

SOC026000 — Social Science / Sociology / General

BUS041000 — Business & Economics / Workplace Culture

FAM027000 — Family & Relationships / Interpersonal Relations

Cover photograph of Judd Allen by Karen Pike of www.kpikephoto.com

Table of Contents

Acknowledgements v
Chapter 1: Discovering the Power of Social Climate in Our Lives 1
Chapter 2: Measuring Your Subculture's Social Climate 15

Part I: Strengthening the Sense of Community 21
Chapter 3: We Care for One Another in Times of Need 29
Chapter 4: We Stay Current on One Another's Activities and Interests 35
Chapter 5: We Have Really Gotten to Know One Another 41
Chapter 6: We Trust One Another 47
Chapter 7: We Feel Comfortable Saying What is on Our Minds 53
Chapter 8: We Look Forward to a Future Together 59
Chapter 9: We Feel a Strong Sense of Belonging 67

Part II: Creating a Shared Vision 75
Chapter 10: We Share Values 83
Chapter 11: We Listen to Each Other 89
Chapter 12: We Make Decisions in Inclusive and Respectful Ways 95
Chapter 13: We Cooperate 103
Chapter 14: We Share Responsibility for Making Things Work 109
Chapter 15: We Have Clear and Consistent Goals 119
Chapter 16: We Are Free to Do Things 127

Part III: Fostering a Positive Outlook 135
Chapter 17: We Maintain High Standards 143
Chapter 18: We Have Team Spirit 149
Chapter 19: We Resolve Conflict in Positive Ways 157
Chapter 20: We Celebrate Achievements 165
Chapter 21: We Have a Can-Do Attitude 173
Chapter 22: We Are Proud 179
Now Is the Time to Strengthen Our Social Climate 187

References **199**

Acknowledgements

My father, Robert F. Allen, Ph.D., was tremendously enthusiastic about three social climate factors: a sense of community, a shared vision, and a positive outlook. Based on our preliminary research, we co-authored a book chapter and a journal article. When my dad passed away in 1987, we had just begun developing and testing approaches to enhance these factors. This book represents the culmination of my father's original vision.

I am grateful to those who have completed the *Social Climate Indicator* over the past 30-plus years, as well as to the many businesses, educational organizations, and community groups that have used the tool to assess their social environments and inform their efforts to strengthen community, shared vision, and positive outlook. Much has been learned from their pioneering efforts.

This book ambitiously explores twenty distinct social climate attitudes and behaviors. My primary role has been to identify the attitudes and behaviors that nurture a supportive social climate and gather information about them. My goals were to offer a diverse range of options for those seeking to enhance the social climate at home, at work, and in the community. I utilized large language models (LLMs) to clarify what is known about these attitudes and behaviors. I am grateful to everyone whose ideas and research findings have been incorporated into the LLMs. This new technology made me feel more like an editor than an author. I have found the research for this book both enlightening and enjoyable.

Thanks to Don Ardell, Michael Arloski, Jim Carman, Bill Hettler, Joe Leutzinger, Tad Mitchell, Michael O'Donnell, Erin Pataky, Gillian Pieper, Kay Ryan, Samia Simurro, Marie Josee Shaar, Elaine Sullivan, and Jack Travis. These leaders share a vision that embodies both organizational kindness and flourishing. My close friends and family generously offered their feedback and encouragement. Mollie Allen, Richard Blount, Diana Parent, Jonathan Sands, Mary Sochet, and Clay Warren were immensely helpful.

Chapter 1
Discovering the Power of Social Climate in Our Lives

Our goal is to create supportive cultural environments in which our need for one another is viewed not as an obstacle to overcome but as a virtue to celebrate.

ROBERT F. ALLEN, PH.D.

THIS BOOK FOCUSES on creating supportive cultural environments that promote health and productivity. It empowers you to collaborate with others to foster uplifting social settings at work, at home, and in your community. It shows that social climate is the key factor that allows our families, friend groups, neighborhoods, and businesses to thrive. This book provides a method for assessing the attitudes and behaviors that shape the social climate. The *Social Climate Indicator* empowers you to concentrate on strategies that will have the greatest impact. Your success with this approach will break down social barriers and transform your culture into one that is vibrant, adaptive, and flourishing.

Chapter 1

Discovering the Culture's Equivalent of Yeast in Baking Bread

My father, Robert F. Allen, founded the Human Resources Institute in the 1960s to empower businesses, government agencies, healthcare organizations, educational institutions, and communities to achieve lasting and positive cultural changes. Since then, our research, publishing, and consulting firm has supported hundreds of culture change projects. While most of our projects focused on business outcomes such as product innovation, teamwork, and productivity, many of our culture change initiatives also addressed broad social issues, including poverty, racism, crime, environmental protection, and unhealthy lifestyle practices.

Cultures and subcultures form intricate webs of social influences on attitudes and behaviors. The primary strands of these cultural webs include (1) shared values, (2) leadership support, (3) peer support, (4) norms, (5) informal and formal policies and practices, and (6) social climate. Cultural webs exist within households, families, peer groups, workgroups, community organizations, and entire nations. My father was a leading expert on changing cultural norms. My initial focus was on mobilizing peer support systems among family, friends, and coworkers. Our work empowered clients to modify cultural aspects that undermine health and productivity.

Just before my father passed away in 1987, we wrote a journal article and a book chapter that examined how social climate influences cultural change, either by fostering or obstructing it. A retrospective study of twenty culture change projects identified the cultural factors that helped organizations and communities succeed in navigating change. We reviewed data from large-scale culture change projects we had been involved in over the previous quarter-century. This study analyzed the key factors that contributed most to the successes achieved. Upon examining the data, three core factors emerged:

- **A sense of community.** The subculture's friendliness factor encompasses caring, trust, openness, a sense of belonging, and a shared belief in a future together.
- **A shared vision.** Members of the subculture are aligned, sharing common values, a unified purpose, and a source of inspiration.
- **A positive outlook.** The culture's "yes, we can" factor encompasses recognizing strengths, celebrating achievements, and transforming challenges into opportunities.

The three social climate factors are the cultural equivalent of yeast in bread making. According to our research findings, where these factors were abundant, individual and collective change flourished, and cooperative action and personal transformation proceeded smoothly. People engaged at high levels, and the intended changes tended to stick. Conversely, where these factors were absent, little constructive change was achieved. Without a supportive climate, individual and collective growth came to a standstill. We were thrilled about these new findings, as it was often puzzling to see how our work thrived in some settings and withered in others.

These findings increased my interest in the seemingly simple yet powerful social climate factors. To illustrate the influence of these cultural forces, I created a movie, *Working Well*, featuring five workgroups with supportive social climates. I found that these factors improve individuals' ability to reach healthy lifestyle goals. Medical research shows that a supportive social climate enhances immunity, longevity, and healing. Business research indicates that cohesive organizations enjoy many benefits, including higher customer satisfaction, greater innovation, and better teamwork.

I now view social climate factors as equally important as the five other cultural influences: shared values, norms, peer support, organizational support, and leadership support. I developed a survey to assess their levels in workgroups. In my work, I closely examine how my clients' efforts enhance or undermine the social climate. My best advice often involves improving the social climate, which seems essential regardless of the overall project goals.

This book shares what I have learned, and I hope it will empower you to strengthen the social climate of your household, workplace, or community. Chapter 2 discusses measuring social climate with a 20-question *Social Climate Indicator*. You and your group can complete this brief assessment to identify your strengths and areas for improvement. Seven questions measure the sense of community, seven questions measure the shared vision, and six questions measure the positive outlook.

The remainder of this book offers an in-depth examination of the social climate, attitudes, and behaviors measured by the *Social Climate Indicator*. Each chapter begins with definitions and examples across various settings, including workplaces, households, and communities. The chapters explain how attitudes and behaviors impact the social climate, identify primary myths and misunderstandings, and suggest strategies for enhancing the impact of attitudes and behaviors on the social climate.

Social Climate Makes a Unique Contribution

Many attitudes and behaviors related to social climate are very familiar. They were once commonly found in daily life. The social climate shares many characteristics with concepts such as teamwork, social capital, and human capital, as well as other ideas in the social sciences. It is often used interchangeably with the term 'culture.' However, as the table below shows, social climate is a distinct social force, set apart by its ability to support individual and organizational change.

Social Climate: Concept Similarities and Differences

Concept	Similarities	Differences
Culture	The social climate is an integral part of culture, serving as an enabling factor that facilitates growth.	Culture is a more comprehensive concept, encompassing additional social factors such as norms, shared values, traditions, and peer support.
Morale	Good morale is like a positive outlook. An upbeat "we can do it" philosophy is also evident in a good social climate.	Whereas morale is a general positive feeling about the group, a good social climate is associated with specific behavior and social norms, such as the norms of getting to know and care for one another.
Teamwork	Teamwork is working collaboratively with a group of people to achieve a goal. It is more likely to exist in a good social climate.	Social climate refers to the overall social atmosphere, whereas teamwork is specifically focused on achieving a goal. It is possible, but less likely, for people to pull together as a team even when enduring a poor social climate.

Chapter 1

Social Capital	Social capital expresses the value of cooperation created through human relationships or networks. Social capital is how an economist might express the value of an excellent social climate. Investing in a good social climate is also an investment in social capital.	Unlike social capital, social climate refers to how cultures facilitate personal and organizational growth. The social climate is expressed through a sense of community, a shared vision, and a positive outlook. Social capital is more closely tied to the impact of relationships on productivity and profitability.
Human Capital	Human capital refers to the stock of skills and knowledge that an individual possesses, enabling them to perform labor and produce economic value. It is the skills and knowledge a worker gains through education and experience.	Whereas human capital is the sum of individual capabilities, social climate is the quality of synergistic social connections. Having a lot of human capital is possible without a good social climate, but in the absence of a good social climate, much of this human capital goes to waste.

A Healthy and Productive Social Climate

Perhaps you have been fortunate enough to experience a group or organization where everything seemed to fall into place. I felt that way during my time as a student activist in the 1970s and 1980s. My fellow students and I were passionate about the need for environmental protection, the end of apartheid in South Africa, stopping mercenary wars in Central America, and securing equal rights for women and LGBTQ+ individuals. We organized film series, published newspapers, held lectures, and staged demonstrations. We sang songs, laughed, and played together, truly caring for one another. Although some tasks, like stuffing envelopes, were monotonous, we all pitched in. Even the occasional conflict with the authorities felt worth the risk.

I've observed that most significant historical achievements have coincided with a supportive social climate. When the Allies defeated fascism, most Americans—both civilians and military—contributed to a common cause. As a boy, I witnessed the Civil Rights and anti-war movements, where adults and youth risked their freedoms for important causes. More recently, I've learned more about Nelson Mandela's remarkable ability to overcome tremendous forces by uniting people in the fight against racist tyranny. These moments shaped lives and told extraordinary stories of how cooperation and creativity can conquer adversity, highlighting the power of community, vision, and a positive outlook.

Similar stories of remarkable artistic and scientific achievements coincide with extraordinary social climates. One of my favorite stories is about how Gertrude Stein organized Saturday evening gatherings at her Paris apartment. These lively gatherings attracted many great artists and writers of the time, including Pablo Picasso, Paul Cézanne, Pierre-Auguste Renoir, Henri Matisse, Henri de Toulouse-Lautrec, Georges Braque, André Derain, Henri Rousseau, Ernest Hemingway, Ezra Pound, Thornton Wilder, and Sherwood Anderson. Another notable instance of a transformative social climate occurred at the Bauhaus, a school in Germany that blended crafts and fine arts, becoming renowned for its design philosophy, which it publicized and taught. It operated from 1919 to 1933 and had a profound influence on subsequent developments in art, architecture, graphic design, interior design, and industrial design.

Social Climate in Everyday Life
Social climate plays a unique role in enhancing everyday life. Have you ever wondered how factory workers, parents, dentists, farmers, and all the rest of us manage to tolerate repeating the same tasks day after day? Most people rely on friendly social interactions to get through the day, looking forward to chatting with their peers over lunch, collaborating to solve problems, and sharing stories. We want to feel a sense of belonging. Many employees are willing to endure low pay and even an unpleasant boss to enjoy the company of their coworkers. A favorable social climate is a primary form of compensation in most work settings. Maintaining such an encouraging social environment is key to recruiting and retaining talent, as it also makes the challenges that often accompany work more bearable.

Maybe You Have a "Popcorn Problem"
I once received a call from the hospital president. His first words were, "Judd, we have a popcorn problem." This puzzled me, so I asked for further clarification. He explained that the nurses enjoy making microwave popcorn, but the patients complain about the smell. He added that the nurses were unwilling to stop. He recognized that the hospital needed the services of a culture expert. He wisely understood that the popcorn problem had deeper roots in the organizational culture.

Upon closer examination, it became clear that the nurses and other hospital staff lacked a cohesive culture that encouraged cooperation and service. In such a "what's in it for me?" atmosphere, why would anyone surrender their popcorn without a struggle or at least some compensation? It turned out that the nurses were not alone in their dissatisfaction; the physicians were also at odds, and many were hesitant to refer their patients to anyone working nearby. The situation was so dire that this community was labeled one of the worst places to get sick in America. Fortunately, no one wished for such unpleasantness, and with some support and creativity, they came together to turn the page. A better social climate significantly enhanced the quality of medical services and the well-being of everyone involved.

Perhaps you, too, encounter the equivalent of popcorn problems within your household, group, or organization. Fewer than 20 percent of long-term personal and organizational goals are achieved. Cultural barriers ultimately overwhelm change efforts, even with inspired leadership and motivated participants. New Year's health resolutions rarely last beyond March. Significant business goals for creating learning organizations, total quality management, and principle-centered leadership begin with great enthusiasm but quickly disintegrate.

Two independent studies, published by Arthur D. Little and McKinsey & Co., found that among the hundreds of Total Quality Management (TQM) program studies, about two-thirds fail to produce the hoped-for results. Reengineering has fared no better; several articles, including some by leading experts, estimate the failure rate at around 70 percent. In a study of one hundred top management-driven "corporate transformation" efforts, Harvard's John Kotter concluded that more than half did not survive the initial phases. He identified a few "very successful" efforts and "utter failures." The vast majority lay "... somewhere in between with a distinct tilt toward the lower end of the scale."

> ### See for Yourself
>
> Next time you're in a group of 10 or more people, ask for a show of hands.
>
> *Raise your hand if you tried to change one or more health practices in the past year. This includes efforts to lose weight, exercise more, manage stress, improve friendships, or any other initiative you may have undertaken for a New Year's resolution or another reason.*
>
> You are very likely to see a vast majority of hands raised. Then, privately, to avoid causing embarrassment, inquire about their successes. How many individuals have fully realized their lifestyle change goals? Listen to their experiences; you will likely hear about ambitious plans and limited progress. Most people will mention that they did not fully achieve their intended goals for more than a short period.

Failure undermines self-esteem and fosters cynicism. Some groups even invent jargon to mock skepticism. At Harley-Davidson, management's latest grand ideas are met with the term "AFP," which is publicly translated as: "Another Fine Program." Insiders understand what the four-letter word beginning with F truly signifies. Frustrated by unsuccessful initiatives, people consistently seek new, more inspiring goals. Some new-age and corporate gurus have proposed bizarre, simplistic, and potentially harmful ideas to distinguish themselves from past failures. Tough love, fad diets, and corporate "right-sizing" serve as reminders of past failed approaches to change. Doctors often prescribe costly and dangerous drugs due to their reluctance to recommend essential lifestyle changes. After all, doctors rightly perceive that few of their patients will successfully implement lifestyle changes.

Hopefully, the groups and organizations you belong to already foster at least moderate levels of a sense of community, a shared vision, and a positive outlook. Have you ever been part of a group that didn't get along? Sadly, almost everyone has experienced hostile social climates at some point. For example, an airport with numerous flight cancellations is often a very negative environment. A household during a contested divorce is another instance. A business undergoing layoffs typically has a challenging social climate. Similarly, a workgroup with an authoritarian boss likely suffers from a toxic social environment.

In such settings, individuals often experience loneliness, despair, hatred, rage, frustration, and fear. Little is accomplished. People long for an escape, finding being alone preferable to confronting the wrath and unpleasantness of others. In these environments, personal abilities are diminished. From a human resources perspective, the whole is less than the sum of its parts.

An unhealthy social climate exacerbates destructive situations. The financial dislocation caused by layoffs, for example, can be devastating. When combined with backstabbing, finger-pointing, and cruelty, it is easy to see why suicides and violence may result. One story that particularly illustrates the destruction inflicted by an unhealthy social climate occurred among the African mountain tribe known as the Ik. Their livelihood was undermined when the government relocated them to a reservation and forbade them from hunting. The Ik had once been known as a kind and peaceful people, but they were transformed into a hateful group. They pushed three-year-old children out of the way and stole food from them. They laughed uncontrollably when misfortune struck. The story of the Ik illustrates how an unhealthy social climate can turn an already challenging situation into a horrific human tragedy.

Recognizing Social Climate at Work, at Home, and in the Community

A strong social climate is crucial for families, workplaces, towns, states, and nations. The following stories illustrate this point. Though the names and places are fictitious, a powerful underlying truth is expressed.

The Power of Social Climate at Brookside Elementary

Brookside Elementary was a place of joy. Students dashed through the halls enthusiastically, and teachers approached each day with passion. The walls were adorned with artwork, the library buzzed with curious minds, and recess echoed with laughter.

As the new school year began, the energy in the staff room felt different—tense, tired, and distracted. Many teachers, already overwhelmed by curriculum changes and administrative tasks, sensed the pressure of larger class sizes and unfamiliar technology for which they had not received training. The positive, can-do attitude that once fueled the school was slipping away.

Where students once arrived with excitement, many now seemed disengaged. Even the school's star pupils appeared less motivated, and behavioral issues were on the rise. The teachers, exhausted and stressed, found themselves less patient. Instead of collaborating to solve problems, they retreated to their corners, trying to survive each day.

The Heart of the Store: Social Climate at The Daily Market

The Daily Market was a neighborhood staple for as long as anyone could remember. It was a small, family-owned grocery store where regulars greeted the staff by name, and kids loved to stop by after school for a snack. While big-box stores surrounded the area, The Daily Market thrived because it had a heart. The store's manager, Mallory, had worked there for almost a decade. She loved her job—connecting with customers, mentoring younger employees, and being part of the local community. The staff weren't just there to sell groceries; they were part of a team with a shared purpose.

Employees felt a strong connection to the store and one another. They collaborated to solve problems, whether addressing demanding customers or finding better ways to manage the workload. Because they felt supported, they had the energy to engage with customers. The Daily Market was more than just a store—it was a community. At the heart of that community was the morale that sustained it all.

The Role of Social Climate in the Rodriguez Family

Like many, the Rodriguez household was a hub of constant activity. The days were full with work, school, and a never-ending list of chores. However, despite the hustle and bustle, their home always remained a warm and welcoming place, where laughter echoed through the halls and family dinners formed the heart of their days.

Maria, the family matriarch, took pride in creating a home where everyone felt loved and supported. Whether cooking her favorite meals or helping her two teenage kids, Sofia and Marco, with their homework, Maria found joy in being the heart of the family. Together, the members of the Rodriguez family brainstormed ways to maintain their family connections. They decided to have a family game night or watch a movie together once a week. During dinner, they would put their phones away so they could focus on talking. Most importantly, they all pitched in to keep the house running smoothly, so no one felt overwhelmed.

Maria realized that home wasn't just a place where people lived; it was a space where they thrived together. A supportive social climate wasn't confined to workplaces or teams; it was the heart of the family. When morale was low, everything—communication, teamwork, and love—suffered. However, when everyone made an effort to uplift each other, the home became a haven of joy and resilience.

The Rodriguez family understands the key to a happy home isn't grand gestures or perfect harmony. It involves being present for one another, listening attentively, and creating opportunities for connection amidst life's chaos. The family's social environment serves as the foundation of their happiness.

Chapter 2

Measuring Your Subculture's Social Climate

IT CAN BE challenging to address complex and abstract cultural phenomena, such as the social climate. To be addressed, the social climate must first be measured. The measures should clarify what it means to achieve a supportive social climate, being broad enough to encompass all dimensions without being so vague that it leaves people scratching their heads, wondering whether the social climate is merely another term for culture. Ideally, the methods should be widely applicable and valuable in household, workplace, and community settings. The results of such measures should be reliable, referring to the consistency and stability of the methods over time, across different groups, and in varying conditions. A reliable measurement strategy yields similar results when the social climate hasn't changed, allowing stakeholders to trust that observed differences are genuine and not due to measurement error. Most importantly, it should be actionable, meaning the results can be used to diagnose needs, set goals, and evaluate progress.

There are several ways to measure a group's sense of community, shared vision, and positive outlook, each offering insight into the underlying concept. One approach is to observe how people behave, including their treatment of one another, whether they are caring and cooperative, and if they celebrate achievements. Another method is to ask open-ended questions about their experiences, enhancing understanding by allowing individuals to elaborate on their perceptions of the group. A third strategy involves conducting field experiments where the group is assigned a challenging task and observed. A fourth measurement method uses surveys, which provide a quick assessment and help break down complex concepts into specific attitudes and behaviors.

The Social Climate Indicator

The Social Climate Indicator is a confidential and anonymous survey designed to measure the sense of community, shared vision, and positive outlook within a group or organization. This 20-item multiple-choice survey can be completed in approximately 10 minutes; however, the time required may be longer if an open-ended question is included, such as "Please share any thoughts, questions, or concerns you may have about the topics covered in the survey." Responses from individual members can be used to estimate the social climate. Averaging responses from all group members provides the most accurate measure of social climate.

Evaluating Your Social Environments

Select any group or organization you are familiar with. Use the following *Social Climate Indicator* to evaluate its sense of community, shared vision, and positive outlook. You can repeat this exercise for all significant groups and organizations in your life, such as your household, neighborhood, religious group, school, or community.

Social Climate Indicator Instructions

The social atmosphere plays a crucial role in the well-being of individuals, groups, and organizations. This confidential and anonymous survey assesses its effects on your group. The survey results will be used to promote a healthier and more productive social environment.

Note: There are no right or wrong answers; we are simply seeking your opinion.

Using the five-point scale, rate your level of agreement with the following statements.

5 Strongly Agree 4 Agree 3 Neither Agree nor Disagree
2 Disagree 1 Strongly Disagree

5 4 3 2 1	We care for one another in times of need.
5 4 3 2 1	We stay current on one another's activities and interests.
5 4 3 2 1	We have really gotten to know one another.
5 4 3 2 1	We trust one another.
5 4 3 2 1	We feel comfortable saying what's on our minds.
5 4 3 2 1	We look forward to a future together.
5 4 3 2 1	We feel a strong sense of belonging.
5 4 3 2 1	We share common values.

5 4 3 2 1   We listen to each other.

5 4 3 2 1   We make decisions in inclusive and respectful ways.

5 4 3 2 1   We cooperate.

5 4 3 2 1   We share responsibility for making things work.

5 4 3 2 1   We have clear and consistent goals.

5 4 3 2 1   We give one another the freedom to do things in our own way.

5 4 3 2 1   We maintain high standards.

5 4 3 2 1   We have a high level of team spirit.

5 4 3 2 1   We resolve conflicts in positive ways.

5 4 3 2 1   We celebrate achievements.

5 4 3 2 1   We have a can-do attitude.

5 4 3 2 1   We are proud of our group.

Scoring *The Social Climate Indicator*

How did your group perform? A supportive social climate is rarely fully abundant or totally absent; most groups have ample opportunities to improve their social climate. The maximum score for the entire *Social Climate Indicator* is 100. Few groups or organizations achieve this ideal. Most groups can utilize the responses from the indicator to identify specific attitudes and behaviors that will enhance their social climate.

If most individual item scores in the *Social Climate Indicator* are three or lower, your social climate is likely undermining health and productivity. Prioritizing improvement of the social climate is essential because a hostile environment can weaken even the most heroic efforts toward constructive change.

Scores of four or five identify the current strengths. Much can be learned from those aspects of a culture that already enhance the social climate. Use the indicator to recognize your existing strengths, defend and build upon them, and consider how they developed, what keeps them alive, and how to maintain these positive cultural influences. Answers to such questions build momentum toward tackling those areas with lower scores (scores of three, two, or one).

Developing Your Strategy for Social Climate

Fortunately, there are numerous ways to strengthen the sense of community, shared vision, and positive outlook. Each of the twenty attitudes and behaviors included in the *Social Climate Indicator* offers an opportunity to improve the social climate. Each attitude and behavior is discussed in a chapter of this book, beginning with definitions and explaining how this element supports the social climate. The chapters debunk common myths and misunderstandings, offer strategies for change, and conclude with a summary of key ideas.

The following table outlines the chapter and page numbers related to the attitudes and behaviors assessed in the *Social Climate Indicator*. Skim through the book, focusing on the chapters that show the most significant promise. Enjoy this process; enhancing the social climate is a life-affirming journey.

Social Climate Factor	Related Book Chapter and Page Number
Sense of Community	
Caring for one another in times of need.	Chapter 3 Page 29
Staying current on one another's activities and interests.	Chapter 4 Page 35

Really getting to know each other.	Chapter 5 Page 41
Trusting one another.	Chapter 6 Page 47
Feeling comfortable saying what is on our minds.	Chapter 7 Page 53
Looking forward to a future together.	Chapter 8 Page 59
Feeling a strong sense of belonging.	Chapter 9 Page 67
Shared Vision	
Sharing common values.	Chapter 10 Page 83
Listening to each other.	Chapter 11 Page 89
Making decisions in inclusive and respectful ways.	Chapter 12 Page 95
Cooperating.	Chapter 13 Page 103
Sharing responsibility for making things work.	Chapter 14 Page 109
Having clear and consistent goals.	Chapter 15 Page 119
Giving one another the freedom to do things in our own way.	Chapter 16 Page 127
Positive Outlook	
Maintaining high standards.	Chapter 17 Page 143
Having a high level of team spirit.	Chapter 18 Page 149
Resolving conflict in positive ways.	Chapter 19 Page 157
Celebrating achievements.	Chapter 20 Page 165
Having a can-do attitude.	Chapter 21 Page 173
Being proud of our group.	Chapter 22 Page 179

PART I
STRENGTHENING THE SENSE OF COMMUNITY

"We are becoming the most connected society in history—and yet we are lonelier than ever."

— *Vivek Murthy*, former U.S. Surgeon General

"Humans have an evolutionary need to live in groups. Belonging to a tribe was once a matter of survival—and in many ways, it still is."

— *Sebastian Junger*, war correspondent and author of *Tribe*

"Human beings are not only social animals but fundamentally group-oriented in the way we develop, learn, and live."

— *Robin Dunbar*, anthropologist and evolutionary psychologist

A SENSE OF community refers to the feeling of belonging, connection, and mutual support that individuals experience within a group. It reflects shared identity, trust, and commitment among members, fostering an environment where people feel valued and understood. The concept of community encompasses several attitudes and behaviors. In a community, there is strong agreement that:

- We care for one another in times of need.
- We stay current on one another's activities and interests.
- We have really gotten to know one another.
- We trust one another.
- We feel comfortable saying what is on our minds.
- We look forward to a future together.
- We feel a strong sense of belonging.

Each of these attitudes and behaviors contributes to the overall sense of mutual connection. How do your social environments foster and sustain a sense of community? Don't be discouraged if your group, organization, neighborhood, family, or household lacks one or more of these elements. We will take a closer look at these community-building attitudes and behaviors in subsequent chapters, examining how to enhance each one.

Sometimes, it is easier to recognize when a sense of community is absent. The lack of community is marked by social and emotional disconnection, where individuals feel unnoticed, unsupported, and isolated. In these situations, people experience:

- **Isolation:** People feel alone, even in groups.
- **Lack of trust:** Individuals are cautious, guarded, or distrustful of others.
- **Emotional disengagement:** There is a lack of empathy, encouragement, and shared emotional experiences.
- **Low participation:** People are less likely to help, collaborate, or get involved.
- **Exclusion or alienation:** Some members feel unwelcome or invisible.
- **Short-term focus:** There is no shared commitment to the group's future or collective well-being.

Community Enhances Productivity

A sense of community plays a foundational role in supporting group and organizational functioning by enhancing connections, cooperation, and commitment among members. It creates the social fabric that enables individuals to work together effectively, adapt to change, and pursue shared goals. The following table outlines several ways in which a sense of community supports group and organizational goals.

- **Strengthens cohesion:** Fosters trust, inclusion, and loyalty, making members emotionally invested in the group.
- **Fosters collaboration:** Encourages mutual support, open communication, and knowledge sharing, thereby breaking down silos and fostering teamwork.
- **Enhances motivation:** Provides a sense of purpose and belonging that motivates people to contribute above minimum expectations.
- **Improves communication:** Fosters a safe environment for members to speak, raise concerns, and share ideas freely.
- **Increases resilience:** Facilitates groups in managing stress, adapting to change, and resolving conflict through trust and shared goals.
- **Drives engagement:** When people feel their presence is valued and matters, they are more likely to participate in meetings and decision-making.
- **Promotes innovation:** When people feel accepted and respected, they're more willing to share creative ideas and take initiative.
- **Supports retention:** Reduces turnover by meeting emotional and social needs that people may not find elsewhere.
- **Aligns values and vision:** Reinforces shared identity and cultural norms, aligning people around common goals and ethical standards.
- **Boosts well-being:** Reduces burnout, stress, and isolation—supporting both individual and collective health, which in turn improves performance.

A sense of community offers numerous benefits for health and well-being. Here are some key findings.

- **Reduced depression and anxiety:** Emotional support and a sense of belonging buffer psychological stress.

- **Greater emotional resilience:** Community helps people cope with trauma, grief, and life changes.
- **Increased self-esteem and optimism:** Feeling valued and accepted boosts confidence and a positive outlook.
- **Lower risk of chronic diseases:** Strong social ties are associated with a reduced risk of heart disease, stroke, and other health issues
- **Improved immune function:** Community reduces stress and strengthens the immune response.
- **A greater likelihood of healthy lifestyle choices:** Social connection encourages physical activity, better diet, reduced smoking, and substance use.
- **Higher engagement with health care:** People are more likely to utilize preventive care and adhere to treatment plans.
- **Lower cortisol levels:** A sense of belonging decreases physiological stress responses.
- **Social buffering effect:** Support from others mitigates the impact of life stressors.
- **Faster recovery from illness or surgery:** Social support improves recovery time and rehabilitation outcomes.
- **Reduced PTSD and trauma-related symptoms:** Community support plays a crucial role in enhancing healing after adverse events.
- **Young people have improved emotional and academic outcomes:** Strong peer and adult connections enhance school performance and well-being.
- **Older adults experience reduced dementia risk, and improved functioning:** Social connection supports brain health and independence.
- **People in recovery experience higher success in addiction treatment:** Community-based support groups (e.g., AA) improve outcomes

Myths and Misunderstandings about the Sense of Community

Several myths and misunderstandings can undermine our ability to strengthen the sense of community. Here are a few of the most counter-productive ones.

Myth/Misunderstanding	Reality
Community happens naturally.	Community often requires intentional design, leadership, and sustained effort, especially in diverse or large groups.
You can't measure a sense of community.	The sense of community can be reliably measured using validated tools.
People just want to do their jobs; they don't care about the sense of community.	Most people value belonging and connection at work and in life, even if they don't express it openly.
A sense of community means everyone agrees all the time.	A sense of community encompasses space for disagreement and diversity, rooted in respect and a shared purpose.
A sense of community is just about being friendly.	It includes additional elements: shared identity, emotional safety, mutual support, and future-oriented commitment.
Remote or hybrid teams can't build community.	While it's more challenging, virtual community-building is possible and increasingly essential.
We have a community because we all work in the same building.	Proximity does not equal connection. People can share space but still feel isolated or excluded.
Community-building is HR's job.	Everyone plays a role. Community is shaped through daily habits, leadership tone, and peer relationships.

Myth/Misunderstanding	Reality
A sense of community is a soft, nice-to-have perk.	It's a core driver of mental health, organizational performance, innovation, and resilience.
Once built, the sense of community will maintain itself.	Community requires ongoing nurturing—like any relationship, it can fade without attention and reinforcement.

Recommended Books on Creating A Sense of Community

Community: The Structure of Belonging, by Peter Block, discusses how to foster inclusive and empowered communities within workplaces and neighborhoods.

Tribe: On Homecoming and Belonging, by Sebastian Junger, explores the psychological benefits of belonging to tightly knit groups, such as military units and indigenous tribes.

The Abundant Community: Awakening the Power of Families and Neighborhoods, by John McKnight and Peter Block, presents an optimistic perspective on how local relationships and citizen-driven engagement can revitalize communities.

Psychological Sense of Community: Research, Applications, and Implications, by David W. McMillan and David M. Chavis, presents the foundational theory and research on the sense of community.

Bowling Alone: The Collapse and Revival of American Community, by Robert D. Putnam, discusses the decline of social capital in the United States and emphasizes the importance of civic engagement and community ties.

Chapter 3

We Care for One Another in Times of Need

CARING FOR ONE another in times of need means offering emotional, practical, and sometimes financial support when someone is facing difficulty, pain, or hardship. It involves recognizing when others are struggling—due to illness, loss, crisis, or stress—and responding with compassion, presence, and action. This care may take many forms, such as listening without judgment, assisting with daily tasks, providing comfort or reassurance, or simply showing up and standing beside someone. At its core, it is an expression of empathy, solidarity, and shared humanity that strengthens bonds and promotes resilience within families, workplaces, and communities. Here are examples of what it means to care for one another in times of need across different settings:

Workplaces

- **Emotional support:** A colleague facing burnout or grief is checked in on regularly, offered flexible deadlines, or given temporary adjustments to their workload.
- **Practical help:** Team members organize meal trains or rides for a coworker recovering from surgery or dealing with a family emergency.
- **Policy-based care:** Leadership offers paid time off, counseling services, or emergency leave to support staff in crisis.
- **Peer solidarity:** Employees voluntarily donate vacation time to a coworker in need or cover shifts without being asked.

Households

- **Family caregiving:** Family members take turns caring for a sick loved one or helping an aging relative with daily routines.
- **Emotional presence:** When one member is going through depression, others listen with empathy, validate their experience, and encourage getting help.
- **Shared burdens:** Partners or housemates redistribute chores or finances during a challenging time, such as unemployment, illness, or childbirth.
- **Affirmation and reassurance:** People express love, patience, and encouragement when someone is overwhelmed or feeling unworthy.

Communities

- **Mutual aid:** Neighbors deliver groceries or prescriptions to elders or those with immuno-compromised conditions during a crisis, such as a pandemic or storm.

- **Community response:** Local groups organize fundraisers or provide support for families experiencing house fires, job losses, or tragedies.
- **Inclusive practices:** Faith groups or neighborhood associations reach out to members in need through support visits, meals, or connection to services.
- **Public rituals of care:** Vigils, memorials, or other collective healing events following local traumas or disasters.

Implications for a Sense of Community

Providing care in times of need powerfully enhances the sense of community within a subculture by fostering trust, emotional safety, and a sense of mutual belonging. When people witness or receive care during hardship, they feel valued and connected, not only as individuals but as part of a group that looks out for one another. These acts of compassion create a culture of reciprocity, where individuals are more likely to support others in return, thereby strengthening social ties. Over time, this fosters a resilient environment where people are more cooperative, engaged, and emotionally invested in the group's well-being. High standards cultivate a climate where individuals expect good things from themselves, each other, and the future. This is also important for a second social climate factor: a positive outlook.

When people do not care for one another in times of need, the subculture often becomes fragmented, distrustful, and emotionally unsafe. Individuals may feel isolated, devalued, or even abandoned, which weakens bonds and erodes the sense of belonging. Without supportive responses during hardship, people are less likely to open up, take interpersonal risks, or invest in relationships. This leads to lower morale, reduced cooperation, and diminished group cohesion.

Over time, the subculture may develop a cold, transactional, or self-protective tone, making it harder to build resilience, resolve conflicts, or mobilize collective effort. The absence of care in critical moments undermines both emotional well-being and the group's long-term strength.

Myths and Misunderstandings about Caring in Times of Need

Myths and misunderstandings about caring for one another can hinder individuals and communities from fully embracing a culture of support and compassion. Here are some common misconceptions along with clarifications to help dispel them:

Myth/ Misunderstanding	Reality
Caring makes people weak or dependent.	Caring fosters resilience. Support during hardship helps people recover faster and become more capable of helping others, not less.
If people need help, they'll ask for it.	Many people feel ashamed, afraid, or unsure about asking for help. In caring cultures, support is offered proactively and compassionately, not just when explicitly requested.
Caring is only for close friends or family.	Healthy subcultures extend care broadly—across coworkers, neighbors, or community members—building trust and inclusion beyond immediate circles.
Caring is too personal for professional or public settings.	When done respectfully and within boundaries, caring strengthens teams, improves morale, and enhances productivity in workplaces and public life.

Myth/ Misunderstanding	Reality
If we care for others, we'll get taken advantage of.	While boundaries are important, most people reciprocate kindness when it's genuine. Cultures of care promote mutual responsibility, not exploitation.
Strong people don't need help.	Everyone needs help at times. Recognizing this truth promotes humility, connection, and emotional health for individuals and the group.
We don't have the time or resources to care for everyone.	Even small gestures, such as listening, checking in, or being flexible, can make a significant difference. When caring becomes a part of the subculture, it transforms into a shared responsibility, lightening the burden for each individual.

Strategies for Fostering a Subculture That Cares

Fostering a caring subculture involves increasing awareness of people's needs and providing ways to help, such as:

- Encouraging open conversations about needs and struggles.
- Creating rituals or norms (e.g., check-ins, "how can I help?" moments) that make support a regular part of group life.
- Modeling compassionate responses from leadership or respected group members.
- Exemplifying vulnerability and a willingness to accept assistance among leaders, elders, and other influential members of the group.
- Establishing buddy systems, care teams, or mutual aid groups.

- Creating flexible policies (e.g., time off, emergency funds, workload sharing) that make caregiving possible.
- Publicly acknowledging acts of kindness and support.
- Including caring as a valued trait in evaluations, promotions, or group celebrations.
- Highlighting real examples where caring made a difference within the subculture.
- Utilizing storytelling to foster a group identity centered on empathy and solidarity.
- Organizing tangible aid (meals, transportation, childcare, donations) for those in need.
- Ensuring that systems of care are accessible and communicated clearly.

Summing Up

A subculture that supports people caring for one another in times of need is one where compassion, empathy, and mutual aid are woven into everyday relationships and group norms. In such cultures, individuals feel safe expressing vulnerability and trust that others will respond with kindness and practical support. This nurturing environment fosters a sense of community by promoting emotional safety, strengthening social bonds, and encouraging mutual responsibility. It creates a shared understanding that no one faces hardship alone, which, in turn, builds group resilience and morale. Achieving this type of subculture requires intentional efforts to normalize helping behavior, build trust, model empathy, and create structures, such as check-ins, support teams, and recognition systems, that make caring visible and sustainable.

Chapter 4
We Stay Current on One Another's Activities and Interests

TO BE CURRENT on activities and interests means staying informed about what the people in your group, such as family members, coworkers, or community members, are doing and what matters to them. This includes:

- Knowing their recent or upcoming activities (e.g., projects, events, hobbies, or travel plans)
- Understanding what they care about, such as goals, passions, challenges, and concerns
- Keeping up with changes in their life circumstances or interests over time

Subcultures where individuals stay updated about one another's activities and interests are characterized by active engagement, attentiveness, and mutual respect. Members of these subcultures consistently strive to understand and acknowledge one another's lives, including their hobbies, milestones, challenges, and daily routines.

This awareness is typically shown through regular check-ins, shared conversations, celebrations of achievements, and offers of support during difficult times. Here's what it looks like in various subcultures:

- In a household, family members regularly ask about each other's day and show up for each other's events or milestones.
- In a workplace, colleagues take an interest in each other's projects and personal news.
- In a community, neighbors stay informed about one another's well-being.

A subculture in which people do not stay updated on each other's activities and interests tends to feel disconnected, indifferent, and impersonal. Without this awareness, relationships remain shallow, and individuals may feel overlooked or unimportant. In households, it may appear as if family members are living parallel lives under one roof, with little conversation or shared experiences. In workplaces, it can lead to a lack of collaboration, missed opportunities for support, and a sense that people are "just doing their jobs" without real team cohesion. In communities, it often results in low participation, minimal trust, and a lack of responsiveness to one another's needs. Over time, the absence of mutual curiosity and engagement can erode the sense of belonging and diminish emotional investment in the group.

Implications for a Sense of Community

Staying informed about each other's activities and interests enhances the sense of community by fostering connection, trust, and mutual investment among members. When individuals feel that others are genuinely aware of and interested in their lives, it signifies belonging, care, and shared identity—key features of a sense of community.

Staying current is a form of relational investment that nurtures the social fabric of a group. Here's how it helps:

- **Promotes empathy and support:** Understanding what others are experiencing enables timely encouragement, celebration, or assistance during difficult times.
- **Reinforces mutual recognition:** People feel seen and valued, which boosts morale and emotional connection.
- **Creates common ground:** Awareness of shared interests or goals fosters collaboration and reduces isolation.
- **Establishes trust and safety:** Continuous personal engagement facilitates open and honest communication.
- **Encourages participation:** When individuals realize that others value their contributions and stories, they are more likely to remain involved and engaged.

Myths and Misunderstandings about Staying Current on Activities and Interests

Myths and misunderstandings about people staying current on activities and interests can undermine efforts to strengthen a sense of community. Here are common myths and misunderstandings about staying informed, along with clarifications to help dispel them:

Myth/Misunderstanding	Reality
It's intrusive or nosy.	When done respectfully and with consent, showing interest communicates care, not intrusion. Trust grows when people feel noticed and valued.

Chapter 4

Myth/ Misunderstanding	Reality
It's only important in close relationships, such as friendships or families.	In workplaces, neighborhoods, and broader communities, this practice fosters a sense of belonging and emotional connection, even among new acquaintances.
People will share if they want to—I shouldn't ask.	Many people need invitations or signs of interest to feel comfortable sharing their thoughts. Asking gently signals that you care and are open to listening.
It's a waste of time or unproductive.	Taking time to connect builds trust, improves communication, and enhances group functioning, which in turn improves productivity and cooperation.
Everyone already knows what's going on.	Without intentional effort, people often remain unaware of each other's lives, especially in fast-paced or fragmented environments.
It leads to gossip or favoritism.	When norms are inclusive and respectful, staying current fosters openness and shared connection rather than division.

Strategies for Cultivating a Subculture Where People Stay Current on Each Other's Activities and Interests

Creating subcultures where people stay current on one another's activities and interests involves fostering open communication, curiosity, and regular engagement. Below are key strategies to help build an attentive and connected environment:

- Make time for "how are you doing?" moments in meetings, group chats, or routines.

We Stay Current on One Another's Activities and Interests

- Use icebreakers or casual prompts to share personal updates.
- Set up communal areas or virtual forums for casual conversation.
- Organize shared meals, coffee breaks, or social events that encourage personal sharing.
- Leaders and other influential group members ask about others' lives and listen actively.
- Show appreciation when people share something personal or meaningful.
- Create newsletters, bulletin boards, or messaging groups where people can share milestones, hobbies, or interests.
- Encourage photo sharing, highlights, and "shout-outs" for achievements or life events.
- Acknowledge birthdays, accomplishments, new projects, or family updates.
- Create rituals or customs for celebrating individual and group milestones.
- Promote questions like "What's new for you?" or "What are you working on lately?"
- Teach active listening skills to help people retain and follow up on others' updates.
- Organize clubs, teams, or events based on common hobbies (e.g., hiking, reading, volunteering).
- Use interest-based activities to build deeper connections.
- Make it clear that sharing is always voluntary and consent matters.
- Cultivate a respectful tone that avoids gossip or oversharing.

Summing Up

Staying informed about each other's activities and interests involves regular updates on what others in a group are doing, enjoying, or experiencing. It reflects a culture of attentiveness, care, and mutual engagement, where people take time to listen, share, and follow up. This practice strengthens relationships, builds trust, and reinforces a sense of belonging by demonstrating that each person matters and is valued, qualities essential to a sense of community. It fosters stronger cooperation, emotional support, and a shared sense of purpose. Cultivating this type of culture requires creating opportunities for informal conversations, encouraging regular check-ins, modeling curiosity, celebrating personal milestones, and promoting respectful listening. When individuals feel genuinely known, they are more connected, committed, and willing to invest in the well-being of the group.

Chapter 5

We Have Really Gotten to Know One Another

To REALLY GET to know one another means developing a deep understanding of each other's values, experiences, preferences, goals, strengths, and struggles. It transcends surface-level interactions or factual knowledge (such as jobs or hobbies) and encompasses emotional insight, empathy, and mutual trust. This depth is cultivated over time through meaningful conversations, shared experiences, consistent presence, and active listening. It involves being curious without judgment, showing vulnerability, and caring enough to remember and reflect on what matters to the other person.

Here are examples of what it looks like to really get to know one another in households, workplaces, and communities:

- In a family, members regularly check in on one another's emotional well-being, not just schedules. A parent knows their child's favorite comfort activity when they're anxious,

and a partner anticipates the other's need for space after a stressful day.
- At work, a manager learns not only what motivates each team member professionally, but also what personal passions drive them. Teammates understand each other's working styles and challenges, such as who prefers quiet mornings or needs support during caregiving obligations.
- In a neighborhood, residents have regular, informal gatherings —on porches or at potlucks—and share life updates. They know who just had surgery, who is looking for work, who loves gardening, and who might feel isolated.

Implications for a Sense of Community

Really getting to know one another transforms a group from a collection of individuals into a connected, caring community. When people know one another, it significantly strengthens the sense of community by deepening trust, empathy, and mutual investment. Here's how it plays a role:

- **Trust and safety:** Knowing others personally enhances confidence that individuals will act with care and reliability, fostering emotional safety and openness within the group.
- **Empathy and support:** When people understand one another's stories, values, and challenges, they are more likely to provide meaningful support and avoid making assumptions or judgments. Those receiving support are much more likely to be open to feedback and less likely to misinterpret feedback as damning criticism.
- **Belonging and inclusion:** Feeling seen, known, and valued strengthens the belief that one belongs—not just as a member, but as a unique individual—within the larger whole.

Myths and Misunderstandings about Caring in Times of Need

Myths and misunderstandings about subcultures where people get to know each other can undermine their positive impact. Here are some common myths and misconceptions about a subculture in which people truly connect:

Myth/ Misunderstanding	Reality
It's invasive or nosy.	A genuine connection respects boundaries and is built on mutual openness and voluntary sharing, rather than pressure or intrusion.
It takes too much time.	Even small, consistent interactions—such as checking in, remembering details, or showing genuine interest—can foster meaningful connections over time.
It will lead to favoritism or the formation of cliques.	When inclusivity is prioritized, deep knowing enhances cohesion and support for everyone, not just a few.
It's not necessary for effective functioning.	While basic functioning is possible without strong connections, deeper relationships foster trust, cooperation, resilience, and long-term success in any setting.
Professional or formal environments shouldn't get too personal.	Humanizing work and community environments enhances morale, loyalty, communication, and productivity, all while respecting boundaries.

Strategies for Fostering Subcultures Where People Get to Know One Another

Opportunities to learn about one another are not always built into day-to-day interactions. People can live and work together for extended periods without ever truly becoming familiar with one another beyond the most basic aspects of each other's lives. Here are strategies for fostering a subculture where people really get to know one another:

- Host check-ins, shared meals, small group gatherings, or story-sharing "campfires" where people can engage in deeper conversations and discuss their values, experiences, and personal interests.
- Leaders and early adopters can create a positive atmosphere by showing genuine interest in others, asking thoughtful questions, and sharing parts of their own experiences to build mutual trust.
- Organize group projects, volunteer activities, or casual social events. Participating together in low-pressure situations allows individuals to learn more about each other.
- Establish welcoming rituals for newcomers, appreciation practices (e.g., spotlighting someone's strengths), and shared celebrations that foster a sense of familiarity and shared identity.
- Establish smaller, more intimate groupings to help overcome barriers to vulnerability. Pairing or clustering individuals for projects, support, or check-ins increases familiarity and fosters deeper, more meaningful connections.
- Ensure that individuals feel secure expressing themselves without fear of judgment. This involves establishing norms for respectful listening, upholding confidentiality, and encouraging diverse perspectives.
- Make it clear that getting to know each other is not just "nice"—it's essential to group success, well-being, and resilience.

Summing Up

A culture that fosters genuine understanding and connection is one in which people take the time to learn about each other's values, experiences, strengths, and challenges in a respectful and caring way. This type of culture fosters authentic relationships, builds trust, and cultivates a strong sense of belonging—key elements for a healthy and resilient community. When individuals feel seen, heard, and valued, they are more likely to contribute, support others, and remain engaged. Such a culture is cultivated through consistent, meaningful interactions; shared experiences; open communication; and leadership that exemplifies curiosity, empathy, and inclusiveness.

Chapter 6
We Trust One Another

A SUBCULTURE CHARACTERIZED by a high level of trust is one in which individuals believe in each other's integrity, reliability, and good intentions. Trust serves as a fundamental glue, fostering open communication, collaboration, and mutual support. Here are examples of what a high-trust subculture looks like in households, workplaces, and communities:

- Family members openly share their concerns, hopes, and mistakes without fear of harsh judgment. Parents trust teenagers to manage their own schedules and finances, and teenagers trust their parents to respect their privacy and support them during challenging times. Conflict is addressed calmly, with the assumption that everyone means well.
- A manager delegates important tasks without micromanaging, trusting employees to follow through. Employees, in turn, feel safe voicing their concerns about problems, suggesting innovations, or admitting errors. Team members share credit and address disagreements with transparency.

- Neighbors exchange keys when traveling, organize block parties or mutual aid efforts, and trust that fellow residents will look out for each other's safety and well-being. Disagreements at community meetings are handled with mutual respect and a fair process.

Subcultures with low levels of trust are marked by suspicion, cautious communication, and a lack of psychological safety. In these environments, people often assume that others have hidden agendas or will act in self-interest rather than for the collective good. As a result, people may shy away from giving honest feedback, hesitate to ask for assistance, and feel isolated or unsupported. Tasks are often micromanaged, decisions are frequently questioned, and collaboration deteriorates under stress. In households, this can show up as secrecy or blame; in workplaces, as low morale and high turnover; and in communities, as disengagement or conflict. Low trust weakens the social fabric, undermines a sense of belonging, and makes it difficult to establish the shared vision and mutual support necessary for a healthy, functioning group.

Implications for a Sense of Community

High levels of trust are essential for fostering a strong sense of community, as they create the emotional safety and confidence needed for meaningful connections, cooperation, and mutual support. When people trust one another, they are more likely to engage authentically, share resources, resolve conflicts constructively, and take collective action toward common goals. Trust reduces fear and defensiveness, allowing individuals to be vulnerable and interdependent—key ingredients in forming genuine bonds. It also facilitates the development of shared norms, the upholding of commitments, and the inclusion of others. In short, trust transforms groups of individuals into cohesive, resilient communities where people feel they belong and matter.

Myths and Misunderstandings about Trust in Subcultures

Here are common myths and misunderstandings about trust in subcultures, along with clarifying insights:

Myth/Misunderstanding	Reality
Trust must be earned over time.	While trust can deepen with experience, people often begin by extending a baseline level of trust, especially in supportive cultures. Trust can be built quickly through small, consistent actions, openness, and respectful behavior.
Trust means always agreeing.	High-trust groups can have disagreements—sometimes strong ones. What distinguishes a high-trust group is the belief that others will engage in good faith and not exploit or harm one another.
Once broken, trust can never be restored.	Trust can be repaired if parties take accountability, express genuine remorse, and engage in restorative actions. Healthy subcultures support the repair of trust, rather than relying solely on punishment or exclusion.
Trust requires complete transparency.	While openness helps, trust does not mean sharing everything. Boundaries and privacy can coexist with trust when people assume respectful intentions and refrain from jumping to conclusions.

Myth/ Misunderstanding	Reality
Trust is either present or absent.	Trust exists on a spectrum and can vary across relationships and situations. Subcultures often have areas of high trust and other areas with lower trust.
Trust happens naturally in close-knit groups.	Familiarity doesn't guarantee trust. High-trust subcultures often result from intentional efforts to foster fairness, integrity, and shared accountability.

Strategies for Cultivating a Subculture Where People Trust One Another

Creating subcultures where people trust one another involves honest communication, following through on commitments, and delivering promised results. Here are strategies for strengthening the level of trust within subcultures:

- Equip people with the necessary skills and resources to fulfill their responsibilities effectively.
- Clearly define roles, responsibilities, and standards.
- Apply rules fairly and fulfill commitments, ensuring everyone is held accountable in a respectful manner.
- Encourage two-way communication: not just giving information, but actively listening to input and feedback.
- Use regular meetings, suggestion boxes, anonymous surveys, and open-door policies to surface concerns and ideas.
- Create an environment where people feel safe to speak up, challenge ideas, and acknowledge struggles without fear of judgment or retaliation.
- Celebrate curiosity, learning, and thoughtful dissent.

- Provide rewards and recognition in a fair manner.
- Address tensions early through respectful dialogue and mediation.
- Avoid backchannel complaints, favoritism, or punitive responses.
- Co-create goals and visions with input from all levels.
- Involve people in planning and decisions that affect them, reinforcing a sense of ownership and belonging.
- Provide time and space for people to build rapport by organizing retreats, team lunches, group projects, and mentorship.
- Teach skills for effective communication, providing feedback, and resolving conflicts.
- Leaders demonstrate honesty, fairness, humility, and consistency while being transparent and acknowledging their errors.

Summing Up

A subculture with trust is one in which people believe in each other's honesty, reliability, and goodwill, creating a foundation for cooperation, mutual respect, and emotional safety. Trust allows individuals to engage authentically, take interpersonal risks, and work together toward shared goals without fear of exploitation or judgment. This fosters a strong sense of community by encouraging openness, inclusion, and shared responsibility, thereby deepening connections and fostering a sense of belonging. Trust is built and sustained through consistent integrity, open communication, fair processes, and a culture that supports accountability, empathy, and mutual care. When trust is present, subcultures become more resilient, cohesive, and capable of navigating challenges together.

Chapter 7

We Feel Comfortable Saying What is on Our Minds

BEING IN A subculture where people feel comfortable expressing their ideas, thoughts, opinions, concerns, and emotions means they can share their thoughts without fear of judgment, ridicule, or retaliation. This kind of environment supports psychological safety, where people trust that they can speak honestly, even when voicing disagreement, sharing vulnerable thoughts, or offering new ideas, and still be respected and valued by others in the group. Such a subculture is characterized by:

- **Respectful dialogue:** People listen actively and respond constructively.
- **Low fear of negative consequences:** Mistakes or differing opinions are not punished.
- **Encouragement of diverse viewpoints:** Dissenting opinions are welcomed as contributions.
- **Norms for open communication:** Honesty is both expected and supported.

Having an open and honest subculture plays an important role in various settings. Here is how it may appear in households, workplaces, and communities:

Households
- Family members discuss their feelings openly, even when they disagree, without fear of being yelled at or dismissed.
- Children are encouraged to ask questions or express their needs, knowing they will not be shamed or ignored.
- Couples discuss challenging subjects such as finances or boundaries in a calm, respectful manner.

Workplaces
- Team members share concerns or ideas in meetings, knowing their input is taken seriously, even if it's unconventional or critical of the team's approach.
- Managers invite feedback and respond constructively, creating a feedback loop that fosters trust and improvement.
- Employees feel safe admitting mistakes, which allows problems to be addressed early and openly.

Communities
- Neighbors speak up about local issues (e.g., safety, development plans) without fear of backlash.
- Community forums or meetings provide space for diverse voices, and those opinions are genuinely considered.
- Civic dialogue is respectful, even when values differ, facilitating cooperation and collective problem-solving.

When subcultures do not promote open and honest communication, people often feel unsafe, silenced, or disconnected. They may withhold their thoughts, suppress concerns, and avoid sharing feedback due to fear—fear of being judged, dismissed, punished, or excluded. This results in a climate of mistrust, guardedness, and disengagement. Such a subculture is characterized by:

- **Avoidance and secrecy:** People keep their thoughts to themselves, especially those that are critical or innovative.
- **Fear of consequences:** Mistakes or dissenting views may be met with ridicule, retaliation, or exclusion.
- **Superficial harmony:** There may be an illusory sense of agreement or calm, concealing deeper tensions.
- **Lack of emotional safety:** People feel anxious about being vulnerable or authentic.
- **Bottled-up resentment:** Unspoken issues accumulate, resulting in conflict or withdrawal.

Implications for a Sense of Community

Open and honest communication is the glue that binds individuals into a true community—one where everyone has a voice, and every voice matters. A subculture that supports open and honest communication strengthens a sense of community by fostering trust, connection, and mutual respect. When people can speak freely, they feel seen, heard, and valued, which deepens emotional bonds and shared identity. It also helps resolve misunderstandings, prevents conflict, and encourages collaboration, all of which are foundational to a cohesive community.

Myths and Misunderstandings about Open and Honest Communication

Several myths and misunderstandings about open and honest communication can undermine the well-being and functioning of a subculture. Dispelling these myths is crucial for cultivating a culture where people can express their thoughts freely. Here are common myths and misunderstandings about this subject, along with clarifying insights:

Myth/ Misunderstanding	Reality
Honesty always leads to conflict.	When communication is respectful, honesty prevents conflict by addressing issues early. It's silence or avoidance that often causes tensions to build.
Encouraging people to speak freely leads to chaos or a lack of control.	Norms of civility and mutual respect can guide structured, open communication. They foster order through shared understanding rather than top-down control.
It's unprofessional or inappropriate to express emotions or personal views.	Thoughtfully expressing emotions or personal perspectives can humanize interactions and strengthen relationships, even in professional settings.
Only extroverts or confident people benefit from open communication.	A truly supportive subculture creates space for everyone, including quieter voices, to feel safe sharing in their own way.
Speaking up is often perceived as a sign of disloyalty or negativity.	People who speak up often do so because they care and want the group to succeed. Encouraging open expression can signal a high level of engagement.
If we let people speak their minds, they'll only complain.	While grievances may surface, people also share ideas, solutions, and appreciation when they know it's safe to do so.

Strategies for Cultivating a Subculture Where People Feel Comfortable Saying What is on Their Minds

There are several strategies for fostering subcultures in which people feel comfortable expressing their thoughts and opinions. Typically, a combination of some of these methods is necessary to achieve lasting and positive changes. Here are some strategies for achieving this goal:

- Actively solicit input from quieter members and validate their contributions to ensure their voices are heard.
- Utilize tools such as anonymous feedback or round-robin sharing to level the playing field.
- Set aside specific times or forums for open dialogue, such as check-ins, listening circles, or team retrospectives.
- Assure people that they will not face penalties for being honest.
- Practice active listening: paraphrase, ask clarifying questions, and avoid interrupting or reacting defensively.
- Regularly ask, "What's working well? What could be better?"
- Publicly acknowledge and appreciate people who take the risk to speak up, especially in tense or uncertain situations.
- Close the loop by showing how feedback leads to action or reflection.
- Focus on solutions, not blame.
- Leaders and respected members speak candidly and respectfully, especially when discussing sensitive topics. Share both successes and mistakes to normalize honesty and vulnerability.
- Discuss guidelines for challenging conversations, such as: "Speak respectfully," "Disagree without attacking," and

"All voices matter." Review and reinforce these regularly in meetings or gatherings.

Summing Up

A subculture that encourages people to express their thoughts openly fosters an environment of trust, authenticity, and mutual respect. In such subcultures, members feel safe sharing their ideas, concerns, and feedback without fear of judgment or repercussions, which is essential for building strong interpersonal connections and a cohesive group identity. This openness not only enhances collaboration and innovation but also empowers people to contribute meaningfully, knowing their voices are valued.

There are several strategies for achieving this level of open communication. Both leaders and members can practice active listening, demonstrate empathy, and create safe spaces where diverse perspectives are welcome. Establishing clear communication channels, promoting psychological safety, and encouraging two-way dialogue are effective strategies for cultivating such a culture. By prioritizing transparency and inclusivity, subcultures can thrive as supportive communities where individuals feel connected, respected, and engaged.

Chapter 8

We Look Forward to a Future Together

When people look forward to a future together, it means they share a sense of hope, purpose, and commitment toward a common path or goal. This mindset reflects optimism and trust in one another, along with the belief that their relationship has meaning and potential over time. Anticipating a future together fosters a stronger bond, a sense of purpose, and greater resilience during challenging times. Looking forward to a shared future typically involves:

- A shared understanding of what they aim to build or become together.
- A sense of belonging, love, loyalty, or camaraderie that makes planning for the future feel worthwhile.
- Coordinated efforts to set goals, address issues, and make decisions that benefit the group.
- Confidence in the group's ability to face challenges and continue to grow together.

Here are examples of what it looks like when people anticipate a shared future in households, workplaces, and communities:

Households
- Planning for future milestones such as vacations, graduations, or retirement together.
- Investing in the home (e.g., renovations, gardens) signifies a commitment to shared living.
- Raising children with shared values demonstrates that the family is working toward a meaningful legacy.
- Supporting one another's personal goals, such as pursuing a degree or changing careers, with the understanding that it benefits everyone.

Workplaces
- Setting long-term goals collaboratively, such as launching a new product or expanding into new markets.
- Offering professional development opportunities and career paths to employees, demonstrating confidence in their long-term contributions and potential.
- Celebrating work anniversaries and promotions reinforces the importance of tenure and loyalty.
- Fostering a culture of innovation or improvement, where employees are excited about what's next and recognize their role in shaping it.

Communities
- Engaging in long-term projects such as building parks, community centers, or sustainability initiatives.

- Establishing traditions and festivals provides residents with something to look forward to and participate in year after year.
- Encouraging civic engagement, where residents regularly vote, attend town meetings, and volunteer because they believe in shaping the community's future.
- Building intergenerational connections, such as mentoring programs or events that include both youth and elders, demonstrates a commitment to all generations.

When people don't look forward to a future together, the group loses its cohesion. Without a commitment to ongoing relationships, individuals may feel disconnected, uncertain, or even cynical about their group's direction. This often leads to short-term thinking, low engagement, and emotional distance. People are less willing to contribute time, energy, or resources when they don't believe the group has a meaningful future. This manifests as apathy, minimal effort, or withdrawal from shared responsibilities. Without a shared future, relationships often remain superficial. People may avoid forming deeper bonds, hesitate to resolve conflicts, or act primarily out of self-interest. In households, this might result in frequent conflicts or the threat of separation. In workplaces, it leads to high turnover and low morale. In communities, people may move away, disengage from civic life, or fail to support local initiatives. Groups may become reactive instead of proactive, focused on surviving day to day rather than building something meaningful. People may become more guarded or suspicious, assuming others will eventually leave or act in self-serving ways.

Implications for a Sense of Community

Anticipating a future together significantly strengthens the sense of community by fostering connection, commitment, and shared purpose. It helps create a more cohesive, resilient, and caring community where individuals are linked not just by present circumstances but by a shared commitment to what they can build together over time. This approach to strengthening the sense of community also plays an important role in supporting the two other social climate building blocks: a shared vision and a positive outlook. When people believe they have a future together, they are more likely to invest emotionally, socially, and practically in the group's well-being. Here's how this outlook enhances the sense of community:

- When people envision staying connected over time, they are more likely to act in ways that maintain relationships, leading to greater honesty, reliability, and cooperation.
- A future-oriented mindset fosters alignment around long-term goals. People feel more motivated to collaborate and contribute because they believe their efforts will ultimately benefit the group.
- Looking forward together creates a buffer against hardship. It helps communities sustain morale and maintain a positive outlook, knowing that challenges are temporary and progress is achievable.
- People care more for one another and for shared spaces when they anticipate staying involved. This results in increased volunteering, helping behaviors, and the adoption of sustainable practices.
- Shared dreams and plans contribute to a collective identity, as people feel "We are in this together," which deepens their sense of belonging and mutual care.

Myths and Misunderstandings about Envisioning a Shared Future

Several myths and misunderstandings can undermine people's ability to look forward to a future together. Dispelling these myths is crucial for cultivating a culture where people want to stay connected. Here are common myths and misunderstandings about this subject, along with clarifying insights:

Myth/Misunderstanding	Reality
It's just about long-term planning.	Envisioning a shared future is also about emotional connection, shared vision, and a sense of belonging. People can plan together without truly feeling hopeful or a sense of belonging.
Stability means stagnation.	Looking forward to a shared future fosters the trust and safety necessary for innovation and adaptation.
Everyone has to agree on the same vision.	People can hold different hopes and roles while still being committed to a shared direction or purpose. Unity doesn't require uniformity.
It happens automatically in close groups.	Without intentional effort, through communication, shared goals, and rituals, groups can drift apart or lose momentum.
It's idealistic or unrealistic.	It's a practical foundation for resilience, trust, and collaboration. People thrive when they believe their efforts contribute to something lasting and meaningful.
Only leaders or visionaries drive the future.	A shared future is built through everyday actions, conversations, and commitments by people at every level.

Chapter 8

Strategies for Cultivating a Subculture Where People Look Forward to a Future Together

Fostering a subculture where people anticipate a shared future involves cultivating a sense of common purpose, trust, and meaningful engagement. Several powerful strategies can create subcultures in which individuals feel hopeful, secure, and motivated to grow and thrive together over time. Below are key strategies that support this:

- Engage everyone in defining goals, values, and hopes for the future. Employ inclusive planning processes to provide people with a sense of ownership.
- Regularly revisit and refine the vision to keep it relevant and motivating.
- Acknowledge achievements—both big and small—as steps toward a shared future.
- Establish traditions that strengthen continuity, such as annual events or group rituals.
- Share stories of success and perseverance that emphasize long-term growth.
- Build deep, lasting connections through mentorship, collaboration, and social events.
- Allow time for people to connect beyond their formal roles.
- Promote trust-building behaviors that demonstrate honesty, empathy, and reliability.
- Provide opportunities for growth, including skill development, leadership roles, or increasing responsibilities.
- Design structures that allow for meaningful participation over time.
- Emphasize how individuals contribute to the group's future.

- Focus on solutions and possibilities, even in the face of challenges. Model adaptability and optimism during transitions or setbacks.
- Promote a positive outlook and confidence in the group's potential.
- Share updates about long-term plans, progress, and next steps.
- Use language that reinforces a sense of continuity, such as "we're building together" and "in the years ahead...").
- Ensure transparency to build trust in the group's direction.
- Ensure participation is accessible and inclusive for all ages, backgrounds, and roles.
- Invite feedback and listen openly, so people feel valued and acknowledged as part of the future.
- Constructively address conflicts to foster a sense of unity.

Summing Up

A subculture in which members look forward to a shared future is one where they cultivate hope, purpose, and a commitment to ongoing relationships and collective goals. This future-oriented mindset enhances the sense of community by fostering trust, emotional connections, and a shared investment in long-term outcomes. It establishes stability, deepens the feeling of belonging, and encourages individuals to contribute to something greater than themselves. Such a subculture does not emerge automatically; it is built through intentional strategies, such as developing shared goals, celebrating progress, nurturing strong relationships, and ensuring inclusive participation. By actively fostering optimism and engagement, groups can create environments that inspire individuals to grow and thrive together over time.

Chapter 9

We Feel a Strong Sense of Belonging

To FEEL A strong sense of belonging means experiencing a deep emotional connection to a group, place, or community where you are accepted, valued, and included. It involves feeling seen and understood by others, knowing that you matter, and having confidence that you fit in without hiding or changing who you are. Key elements of a strong sense of belonging include:

- **Acceptance**: You feel welcomed and embraced for who you are.
- **Inclusion**: You're actively involved, and your presence is acknowledged.
- **Support**: Others care about your well-being and are responsive to your needs.
- **Shared identity or purpose**: You see common values, goals, or interests with others in the group.
- **Emotional safety**: You can express yourself without fear of rejection or judgment.

Chapter 9

A strong sense of belonging manifests in diverse ways within households, workplaces, and communities:

Households
- Family members feel safe expressing their emotions, sharing their struggles, and being themselves without fear of criticism or rejection.
- Shared routines and rituals—such as mealtimes, celebrations, or regular check-ins—reinforce togetherness.
- Everyone's voice, including that of children, is considered in decisions affecting the household.
- Members consistently express appreciation, offer hugs, say "I love you," or acknowledge each other's efforts.

Workplaces
- Employees from diverse backgrounds feel that their contributions are valued and respected.
- People support one another, celebrate victories together, and care about each other's success.
- Employees feel at ease sharing ideas, concerns, or mistakes without fear of ridicule or punishment.
- Leaders articulate a vision for the future that demonstrates how employees are vital to the organization's success.

Communities
- Newcomers are welcomed, encouraged to participate, and assisted in integrating (for example, through neighborhood gatherings, local clubs, etc.).

- Neighbors help out during times of need, showing each other that they are cared for and not alone.
- Diverse traditions and holidays are respected and celebrated together, showing everyone that their identity matters.
- People feel that their voices matter in local decisions and see themselves represented in leadership or community initiatives.

To lack a sense of belonging means feeling unseen, excluded, or disconnected from those around you. It is the emotional experience of not fitting in, not being valued, or not feeling safe to be yourself in a particular environment. When people experience a lack of belonging, they:

- Feel lonely even when in the company of others.
- Feel that one's presence, ideas, or identity are not acknowledged or welcomed.
- Feel like an outsider, as if you are different in ways that hinder complete acceptance.
- Refrain from expressing thoughts, emotions, or identity because of fear of rejection or judgment.
- Question their value or assumption that they are not good enough to belong.

Implications for a Sense of Community

A feeling of belonging is a cornerstone of a strong sense of community. When people feel they belong, they are more likely to identify with the group, engage positively, and invest in its well-being. Belonging transforms a group from a collection of individuals into a connected, caring, and cooperative community.

Chapter 9

Myths and Misunderstandings about Feeling a Sense of Belonging

Several myths and misunderstandings about a sense of belonging can undermine the well-being and functioning of a subculture. Dispelling these myths is crucial for cultivating an environment where people feel they belong. Here are some common myths and misunderstandings about this subject, along with clarifying insights:

Myth/ Misunderstanding	Reality
Belonging happens automatically.	Simply being part of a group doesn't guarantee a sense of belonging. Belonging grows through consistent inclusion, empathy, and the development of meaningful relationships.
Belonging means fitting in.	Belonging is not about conforming; it's about being accepted and valued for who you truly are. "Fitting in" often involves changing to gain acceptance, whereas true belonging allows for individual differences to be acknowledged and valued.
If someone is quiet or keeps to themselves, it's often because they don't want to be a part of a group.	Some people may be reserved due to past exclusion, social anxiety, or a lack of being welcomed, not a lack of interest. It's important not to confuse silence with disinterest.
Belonging is only about individual effort.	While individuals can take steps to connect, belonging is fundamentally a relational and cultural process. It requires mutual openness and a welcoming environment created by the group.

Myth/ Misunderstanding	Reality
Everyone feels like they belong in inclusive groups.	Even in well-intentioned groups, people from underrepresented or marginalized backgrounds may feel excluded if their identities, experiences, or contributions are overlooked.
Belonging is a "soft" concept.	Belonging has real, measurable impacts on health, performance, and group cohesion. It's critical for mental well-being, learning, productivity, and resilience.
A sense of belonging is permanent once established.	Belonging is dynamic. It can strengthen or erode based on ongoing interactions, leadership changes, inclusion practices, or life transitions.

Strategies for Cultivating a Subculture Where People Feel They Belong

Creating a subculture in which people feel a sense of belonging involves practices that foster inclusion, emotional safety, and a shared identity. Here are strategies to cultivate such a subculture:

- Use inclusive language like "we," "us," and "together."
- Engage in group rituals or traditions that reinforce collective identity.
- Provide opportunities for informal connections, such as shared meals, social events, or team check-ins.
- Pair or group people in ways that help them get to know each other more deeply.
- Encourage mentorship or buddy systems.
- Encourage respectful listening and validate diverse perspectives. Actively invite input from all members, especially those who may feel marginalized.

- Avoid cliques, favoritism, and exclusive language or traditions.
- Notice and address signs of social withdrawal or exclusion.
- Act quickly to resolve conflicts or misunderstandings in constructive ways.
- Regularly check in with individuals to see how they're feeling in the group
- Acknowledge individual contributions publicly and privately.
- Use people's names, remember details about their lives, and show appreciation.
- Celebrate both personal milestones and group achievements.
- Create emotionally safe spaces where people can be themselves without fear of judgment.
- Normalize vulnerability by modeling openness and self-disclosure.
- Avoid pressuring people to "fit in" by changing who they are.
- Establish and revisit shared values, goals, and vision.
- Adapt activities, events, and communication methods to ensure that everyone can participate.
- Be mindful of potential barriers regarding language, schedules, transportation, and cultural practices.
- Ensure that people in leadership and decision-making roles are open and representative.
- Share stories and practices that reflect the importance of belonging.
- Reinforce a sense of belonging by recognizing people's contributions and including group members in rituals.

Summing Up

When members of a subculture feel a strong sense of belonging, they feel accepted, valued, and connected to others in meaningful ways. This emotional bond fosters trust, inclusion, and a shared sense of identity, which are essential to building and sustaining a strong sense of community. Belonging motivates individuals to engage fully, support one another, and take collective responsibility for the group's well-being. It is achieved by creating an environment where people are welcomed as they are, where diverse voices are heard and respected, and where relationships are nurtured through consistent recognition, shared purpose, and inclusive practices. A subculture rooted in belonging lays the foundation for a community that is emotionally resilient, cooperative, and united.

PART II
CREATING A SHARED VISION

A SHARED VISION is a common and inspiring image of the future that a group agrees upon and collectively works toward. With a shared vision, people have similar mental pictures of what success looks like. They find the vision inspiring and use it to guide decisions, attitudes, and behaviors. They believe that the vision is widely held among other members of the group. The vision is shared in that it is mutually agreed upon, emotionally resonant, and collectively pursued. People are given the freedom to contribute. A shared vision encompasses multiple attitudes and behaviors, such as:

- We share common values.
- We listen to each other.
- We make decisions in inclusive and respectful ways.
- We cooperate.
- We share responsibility for making things work.
- We have clear and consistent goals.
- We give people the freedom to do things their way.

Each of these attitudes and behaviors contributes to the shared vision. How are your social environments helping to build and maintain a shared vision? Don't be discouraged if your group, organization, neighborhood, family, or household lacks one or more of these elements. In subsequent chapters, we will examine each of these attitudes and behaviors and discuss how to strengthen them.

Organizations often lack a shared vision, particularly during periods of rapid change, leadership turnover, or significant growth. Only 22% of employees strongly agree that their organization's leadership has a clear direction for the organization (Gallup, 2023). Research and real-world experience suggest that while most organizations have a vision statement, few have a truly shared vision that everyone understands, embraces, and acts upon.

Without a shared vision, an organization or group lacks a cohesive sense of purpose, making it difficult to move forward effectively or sustainably.

Groups and Organizations Benefit from a Shared Vision

A shared vision serves as a unifying force that aligns efforts, boosts morale, and drives meaningful progress. Here's a list of some of the many benefits:

- **Alignment and focus:** People work toward the same goals, reducing duplication and conflict. A common direction guides decisions and strategies..
- **Motivation and engagement:** People feel energized and committed when they believe in a meaningful future. A shared vision taps into intrinsic motivation.
- **Collaboration and teamwork:** A shared purpose builds trust, reduces competition, and strengthens cooperation.
- **Innovation and initiative:** People are more likely to take creative risks and propose solutions when they understand how their contributions contribute to overall goals.
- **Resilience and adaptability:** A shared vision helps teams stay grounded and unified during change, setbacks, or uncertainty.
- **Identity building:** A shared vision fosters a sense of purpose, pride, and shared responsibility, contributing to a strong organizational identity.
- **Performance and results:** Studies have found that individuals with a shared vision tend to outperform those without one.
- **Attracting and retaining talent:** A shared vision is appealing to people seeking meaning. This helps with hiring and keeping top talent.

Health and Well-being Benefits from a Shared Vision

A shared vision nurtures well-being by meeting deep psychological needs for meaning, connection, hope, and coherence. It transforms work and group interactions from a source of stress into a source of health. Much of the research explores the psychological benefits of a shared vision; however, it is also evident that emotional well-being improves other health outcomes. Shared purpose, clarity, and connection fulfill core psychological needs—and these, in turn, influence physical health in measurable ways. Gallup and WHO studies show that purpose-aligned teams are healthier. A shared vision reduces uncertainty and role conflict, thereby enhancing predictability and control, key factors in lowering stress. People in settings with shared visions have lower rates of heart attacks and strokes. Several biological pathways help explain these health benefits. A shared vision has been found to:

- Lower cortisol by reducing threat perceptions.
- Enhance dopamine and oxytocin, which promote motivation and bonding.
- Reduce sympathetic nervous system overload, protecting against inflammation and wear-and-tear (allostatic load).

Myths and Misunderstandings about a Shared Vision

There are several myths and misunderstandings about shared vision that can limit its effectiveness or prevent organizations from building one at all. Believing these myths can lead to weak or performative visions that fail to inspire. These misconceptions often confuse a shared vision with slogans, top-down directives, or passive agreement, when, in fact, a shared vision is a living, evolving force that requires active participation.

Myths and Misunderstandings about Shared Vision

Myth/Misunderstanding	Reality
A vision statement = shared vision.	A written statement alone doesn't create shared commitment. A shared vision is only real when it lives in the hearts and actions of people. People must have ways to "walk the talk" and see the vision in practice.
Leaders decide the vision.	Top-down visions rarely inspire ownership. True shared vision is co-created through dialogue, reflection, and collaboration.
Once we have a shared vision, we're done.	Shared vision requires ongoing reinforcement, storytelling, and alignment. It evolves and must be re-engaged on a regular basis.
Everyone must agree on everything.	Shared vision doesn't mean uniformity of thought. It means agreement on key direction and purpose, even with diverse perspectives.
It's too soft or idealistic.	Research findings indicate that a shared vision drives performance, innovation, and resilience when tied to specific goals.
A shared vision is only for leadership or strategy teams.	Everyone in the organization benefits from and contributes to a shared vision. It should guide daily decisions at all levels.
We don't need a shared vision—people already know their jobs.	Tasks and roles alone are insufficient to inspire sustained engagement. A shared vision connects tasks to purpose and fosters long-term motivation.

Myth/Misunderstanding	Reality
A vision statement = shared vision.	A written statement alone doesn't create shared commitment. A shared vision is only real when it lives in the hearts and actions of people. People must have ways to "walk the talk" and see the vision in practice.
Leaders decide the vision.	Top-down visions rarely inspire ownership. True shared vision is co-created through dialogue, reflection, and collaboration.
Once we have a shared vision, we're done.	Shared vision requires ongoing reinforcement, storytelling, and alignment. It evolves and must be re-engaged on a regular basis.
Everyone must agree on everything.	Shared vision doesn't mean uniformity of thought. It means agreement on key direction and purpose, even with diverse perspectives.
It's too soft or idealistic.	Research findings indicate that a shared vision drives performance, innovation, and resilience when tied to specific goals.
A shared vision is only for leadership or strategy teams.	Everyone in the organization benefits from and contributes to a shared vision. It should guide daily decisions at all levels.
Families, neighborhoods, and teams don't need a shared vision—this is exclusively an organizational responsibility.	A shared vision is important for all subcultures. It is an important component of a healthy and productive social climate.

Books about Shared Vision

Here are several highly regarded books that explore the concept of shared vision, its development, and its transformative power in organizations and communities. These books approach the topic from the perspectives of leadership, systems thinking, organizational psychology, and community building.

The Necessary Revolution, by Peter Senge et al., focuses on how a shared vision can drive sustainability and collaborative action for global change.

Built to Last: Successful Habits of Visionary Companies, by Jim Collins and Jerry Porras, shares how enduring companies define and preserve core values while adapting to change. The book emphasizes shared values as foundational.

The Culture Code: The Secrets of Highly Successful Groups, by Daniel Coyle, reveals how shared values — such as safety, purpose, and belonging — are cultivated in high-performing teams and organizations, with great real-world stories.

Chapter 10

We Share Values

SHARING COMMON VALUES in a subculture means that members of that group or community hold similar beliefs about what is important, desirable, and worthwhile. These shared values serve as guiding principles that shape behaviors, decisions, and interactions within the group, helping to define what is acceptable, what is unacceptable, and what is admirable. This fosters a sense of unity and predictability. In a subculture lacking common values, individuals often struggle to agree on what is important, acceptable, or worth striving for within the group.

Here are examples of subcultures that share common values:

- In a family that values open communication, kindness, and mutual support, family members regularly discuss their day, listen to each other, and offer help when someone is struggling. Decisions are made collectively, and members are encouraged to express themselves in a respectful manner. Children grow up with a strong sense of emotional safety and responsibility.

- In a company that values collaboration, innovation, and integrity, team members share credit, support each other's growth, and brainstorm new ideas openly. Leaders reward honesty, ethical decision-making, and taking initiative. Employees feel they contribute to a greater mission and take pride in their organizational culture.
- In a neighborhood that values inclusiveness, safety, and civic involvement, residents actively participate in local events, volunteer for cleanup days, and warmly welcome newcomers. There is strong support for schools, local businesses, and mutual aid efforts. Disagreements are resolved through constructive dialogue, and shared values help guide local decisions.

Implications for a Shared Vision

Shared values are the compass; a shared vision is the destination. Together, they ensure that the path forward is meaningful, coherent, and collectively embraced. When people hold common beliefs about what matters most, it becomes easier to define a future they can work toward together. Here are the key implications:

- Shared values help group members agree on priorities, making it easier to define goals and pathways that reflect everyone's deeper motivations.
- When values are shared, people are more likely to trust one another's intentions and collaborate effectively. This fosters unity and minimizes resistance to change.
- People are more committed to a shared vision when it aligns with their personal and group values, which enhances intrinsic motivation and fosters long-term engagement.

- Shared values establish a common ethical framework for resolving disagreements, facilitating the maintenance of unity even when challenges arise.
- When a shared vision is grounded in enduring values, the subculture can adapt more effectively to change while maintaining its core identity.

Myths and Misunderstandings about Shared Values

Several myths and misunderstandings can undermine the benefits of shared values.

Myth/ Misunderstanding	Reality
Shared values mean everyone thinks the same way.	Shared values create *common ground*, but they don't erase individual perspectives or diversity of thought. People can agree on core principles (like respect or fairness) while still holding varied opinions, backgrounds, and approaches.
Shared values automatically lead to harmony.	While shared values can foster cohesion, conflict still arises, especially when individuals interpret or prioritize values differently. Disagreements are natural, and shared values help guide how conflicts are managed, rather than eliminating them.
Shared values are always explicit and consciously agreed upon.	Many shared values operate implicitly—people absorb them through norms, stories, and behaviors, without formal discussion or explicit instruction. Sometimes, members aren't even aware of the values they share until they're challenged.
Once established, shared values stay the same.	Values can evolve as the subculture grows or faces new challenges. Shifts in leadership, membership, or societal changes can lead to realignments of values.

Myth/ Misunderstanding	Reality
Declaring values (on paper or in slogans) means they are truly shared.	Values are not shared just because they're written in a mission statement. They need to be reflected in consistent actions, decisions, and reinforcement across the group.
Shared values mean external values are rejected.	A subculture can hold shared values while its members simultaneously respect or incorporate values from broader cultures or other groups to which they belong.
All members fully embody the shared values at all times.	In healthy and productive subcultures, individuals may occasionally fall short of shared values. What matters is how the group addresses those gaps through support, feedback, or corrective action.

Strategies for Developing and Maintaining Shared Values

Developing and maintaining shared values in a subculture requires intentional strategies that embed these values into both the formal and informal fabric of the group. Strategies include:

- **Collaborative value discovery:** Engage members in identifying and articulating the values they currently hold or aspire to together. This fosters buy-in and ensures the values reflect the group's genuine priorities. Techniques for value discovery include discussions, surveys, focus groups, and storytelling, which are used to identify common themes.
- **Leadership modeling:** Leaders must consistently model shared values through their actions, decisions, and communication. Leadership behavior establishes the tone

for what is genuinely valued. Effective leadership modeling strategies include highlighting leader actions that reflect values (e.g., transparency in decision-making) and providing mentorship and coaching that align with those values.

- **Embed values in policies and practices:** Align organizational or group policies, procedures, and practices with shared values to ensure their reflection in daily operations. Techniques for this approach in the workplace include integrating values into performance reviews, hiring practices, and rewards; developing guidelines or codes of conduct that embody these values; and designing workflows or decision-making processes that uphold key values.
- **Regular reflection and dialogue:** Maintain visibility and dynamism of values through ongoing conversations and reflections on their effective practice. Techniques for this include conducting periodic "values check-ins" or review sessions, creating safe spaces for open feedback and dialogue, and utilizing case studies or recent scenarios to assess value alignment.
- **Storytelling and recognition:** Utilize stories and recognition to celebrate instances of members embodying shared values, making these values tangible and relatable. Techniques for this approach include sharing success stories in meetings, newsletters, or internal platforms, as well as acknowledging individuals or teams who exemplify core values through formal awards or informal shout-outs.
- **Onboarding and Training:** Introduce new members to shared values consistently and early, ensuring alignment from the outset. Techniques for this approach include highlighting values in onboarding sessions and materials, providing training that connects daily tasks to core values

(e.g., role-playing scenarios), and pairing new members with mentors who embody these values.
- **Encourage peer accountability:** Foster a culture where peers hold each other accountable for embodying shared values. The techniques for this approach include establishing norms for respectful feedback, utilizing peer coaching or buddy systems, and promoting open discussions when values are challenged or conflict arises.
- **Adaptation and evolution:** Allow space for values to evolve as the subculture grows or changes. Revisit and refresh values periodically. Techniques for this approach include conducting periodic value reassessments, integrating feedback from new members or changing environments, and using external trends or challenges as reflection points.

Summing Up

Shared values in a subculture refer to the deeply held beliefs and principles that guide the thoughts, feelings, and actions of its members within the group. These values foster a sense of unity and purpose, laying the cultural foundation for a shared vision. When people align on what matters most—such as fairness, responsibility, or kindness—they are more likely to support common goals and work together to shape a desired future. Shared values foster trust, reduce conflict, and enhance motivation, making collaboration more effective and sustainable. Achieving shared values involves intentional dialogue, inclusive participation, and consistent modeling of those values by leaders and peers. Through reflection, storytelling, and group agreements, subcultures can actively cultivate and reinforce the values that support a strong, unifying vision.

Chapter 11

We Listen to Each Other

WHEN THERE IS a shared vision, people feel heard. In a subculture with a shared vision, there are strong norms for listening. Listening means more than just hearing words—it's about actively engaging with the speaker and being fully present. This type of listening is sometimes referred to as active listening. It typically involves:

- Putting aside distractions, such as phones and thoughts about what to say next, and focusing entirely on the speaker.
- Maintaining eye contact and open body language that signals attentiveness.
- Paying attention to the tone of voice, emotions, and body language.
- Picking up on underlying feelings or unspoken concerns.
- Confirming understanding by summarizing what the other person said ("So what I hear you saying is…").

- Asking thoughtful questions to deepen understanding, not to challenge or interrupt.
- Acknowledging the speaker's feelings and perspectives, even if you disagree.
- Using affirming responses like nodding or saying, "I can see how that would be hard."

Here are examples of how listening is experienced in households, workplaces, and communities:

Household
- Check-ins happen regularly, with everyone taking turns to share and listen.
- Parents model active listening to children's feelings and thoughts.

Workplaces
- Managers consider employee input before providing direction.
- Ideas are not acted on until all voices have been heard.

Communities
- Community meetings begin with listening sessions, followed by discussions of action items.
- Community members listen without interrupting.

Implications for a Shared Vision

When a group engages in active listening, confusion and conflict are less likely to arise. Problem-solving, teamwork, and creativity are more likely to flourish. Conflicts tend to be resolved more amicably; listening helps de-escalate tensions by making people feel heard and understood. Without active listening, a shared vision can easily become fragmented, misunderstood, or rejected. Here's why listening plays such a central role:

- A shared vision often requires ongoing dialogue, feedback, and flexibility, all of which are made possible by listening.
- Listening allows everyone's perspectives, concerns, and aspirations to be heard, which helps align individual goals with the collective vision.

When people perceive that their input is acknowledged, they are more inclined to accept and endorse the vision because their ideas are incorporated into it; they feel like contributors instead of passive followers. This can enhance motivation and long-term commitment. Other benefits of listening include:

- Building trust and psychological safety, encouraging people to contribute ideas and commit to the shared vision.
- Demonstrating respect and valuing others' input, which strengthens group cohesion.
- Revealing diverse viewpoints, experiences, and insights that enrich the shared vision, making it more robust and adaptive. A vision shaped by varied inputs tends to be more innovative and better suited to real-world challenges.
- Clarifying expectations, meanings, and intentions, reducing the risk of misunderstandings that could derail the vision. It ensures that everyone interprets the vision similarly and understands their role in achieving it.
- Ensuring that the vision remains relevant and effective. Active listening enables leaders and groups to adjust strategies when circumstances change or new challenges arise.

Myths and Misunderstandings about Listening

Numerous myths and misunderstandings about listening can hinder genuine connection. Here are some of the most common:

Myth/Misunderstanding	Reality
Listening is passive.	Authentic listening is an active process that requires effort. It involves attention, reflection, empathy, and sometimes setting aside your thoughts and reactions to understand the speaker fully. Passive listening (just hearing without engagement) often leads to misunderstandings.
Listening means staying silent.	While silence can be a part of good listening, active listening includes responses such as paraphrasing, asking clarifying questions, and providing verbal cues ("I see," "Tell me more"). Silence alone doesn't guarantee understanding; it's the thoughtful engagement that counts.
If I'm not giving advice, I'm not helping.	People often want to feel heard and understood, not fixed. Jumping to advice or solutions too quickly can come across as dismissive of the speaker's emotions or experience. Sometimes the best help is holding space for someone to process their thoughts.
Listening means agreeing.	You can fully listen and understand someone's point of view without agreeing with them. Listening is about respect and understanding, not about giving up your own beliefs.

Myth/Misunderstanding	Reality
Multitasking doesn't affect listening.	Trying to listen while checking your phone, thinking about your to-do list, or preparing your response weakens your ability to fully grasp what's being said. The speaker often feels this lack of presence.
You can tell how well you listen.	Many people overestimate their listening skills. Research has found that most people believe they are better listeners than they are (this is a version of the Dunning-Kruger effect). You can close this gap by getting feedback on your listening skills and consciously practicing listening.
Listening ends when the person stops talking.	Sometimes what isn't said is just as important as what is said. Good listeners reflect afterward, consider the emotional subtext, and may follow up thoughtfully.

Strategies for Improving Listening

Improving listening within a subculture involves shaping the norms, expectations, and practices that support active, respectful communication. Here are some strategies for improving the listening culture:

- Make it clear that active listening is expected and valued within the group.
- Conduct workshops or short training sessions to teach active listening skills.

- Establish clear ground rules for communication during meetings or discussions. For example:
  - One person speaks at a time.
  - No interrupting.
  - Summarize what was heard before responding.
  - Use round-robin formats to ensure everyone is heard.
- Get feedback about listening. You can ask:
  - Did everyone feel heard?
  - Were there moments of misunderstanding?
- Leaders and influencers within the subculture can model good listening.
- Acknowledge and celebrate good listening.

In Summary

When people listen to each other, they engage in attentive, empathetic, and open-minded communication. This involves active listening, which goes beyond merely hearing words. Active listening includes focusing on the speaker, understanding their message, and responding thoughtfully. Such engagement fosters trust, reduces misunderstandings, and enhances collaboration. In the context of a shared vision, active listening ensures that team members feel heard and valued, promoting a sense of inclusion and mutual respect. This collective understanding aligns individual efforts with the organization's goals, facilitating cohesive progress and innovation. You can cultivate a culture that values listening by leading by example, providing training, promoting open communication, establishing feedback channels, and rewarding effective listening.

Chapter 12
We Make Decisions in Inclusive and Respectful Ways

MAKING DECISIONS IN inclusive and respectful ways means ensuring that all relevant voices are heard, valued, and considered throughout the decision-making process. It's about fostering fairness, mutual respect, and shared ownership of outcomes. Here's a breakdown of what it means, why it matters, and how to do it well:

Principles for Making Decisions	How to Do It	Why It Matters
Inclusion of Diverse Perspectives	Actively seek out and incorporate input from individuals with diverse backgrounds, experiences, roles, and perspectives.	Diverse input leads to better decisions, greater creativity, and fewer blind spots. It also fosters equity.

Respect for Each Person's Voice	Treat each contributor's opinion with dignity, acknowledging their input without judgment or dismissal.	Respectful engagement strengthens psychological safety, encouraging honest contributions.
Transparency in Process	Clearly communicate how decisions will be made (e.g., consensus, majority vote, leadership decides after consultation).	Helps manage expectations and prevents feelings of exclusion or betrayal.
Shared Power	Ensure that no one person or group dominates. Distribute influence fairly, especially for those who may be marginalized.	Prevents groupthink, empowers participants, and fosters commitment to the final decision.

A Process for Making Major Decisions

A major decision in a subculture refers to a choice or determination that significantly impacts the shared practices, norms, values, relationships, or direction of that specific group. These decisions often shape the identity, priorities, and functioning of the subculture. For instance, in households, major decisions could include choosing to move to a new location, deciding on parenting approaches, or managing shared finances. In workplaces, major decisions encompass establishing core values, setting organizational goals, or changing how team members collaborate. In a community, major decisions involve determining how resources are allocated, setting priorities for shared spaces, or forming coalitions to tackle community issues. Major decisions frequently benefit from a step-by-step approach.

1. **Identify the Decision Context:** Clearly define the issue at hand and its impact on various stakeholders.
2. **Assemble a Diverse Group:** Include individuals from different backgrounds, roles, and experiences relevant to the decision.
3. **Establish Ground Rules:** Set norms that promote respectful dialogue, active listening, and equal opportunity to contribute.
4. **Facilitate Open Dialogue:** Encourage sharing of ideas and concerns, ensuring that all voices are heard and considered.
5. **Synthesize Input:** Identify common themes and divergent viewpoints to inform a well-rounded decision.
6. **Make the Decision Collaboratively:** Aim for consensus where possible, or use agreed-upon methods to reach a decision that reflects the group's input.
7. **Communicate the Outcome:** Share the decision and its rationale with all stakeholders in a transparent manner.
8. **Review and Reflect:** After implementation, assess the impact of the decision and gather feedback to inform future processes and decisions.

When inclusive and respectful decision-making processes fail, they can lead to significant organizational and interpersonal challenges. These failures often result in reduced trust, lower engagement, and suboptimal outcomes.

- **Erosion of Trust and Morale:** When individuals feel their perspectives are disregarded, it can lead to decreased trust in leadership and lower team morale.
- **Groupthink and Suppressed Dissent:** A lack of diverse viewpoints can foster groupthink, where the desire for consensus overrides critical evaluation, leading to flawed decisions.

- **Reduced Innovation and Creativity:** Excluding diverse perspectives limits the range of ideas and solutions, stifling innovation and adaptability.
- **Increased Conflict and Miscommunication:** Failing to include all stakeholders can lead to misunderstandings and conflicts, as decisions may not adequately reflect the needs and concerns of all parties.
- **Disengagement:** People who feel unheard or undervalued are more likely to disengage or leave the organization.

Implications for a Shared Vision

Inclusive and respectful decision-making is essential for fostering a shared vision, as it enhances alignment, commitment, and trust, ensuring that the vision is not merely imposed from above but genuinely shared and embraced by those involved. Here's how:

- When decisions are made inclusively and respectfully, people feel heard and appreciated, which increases their emotional investment in the shared vision.
- People are more likely to commit to a vision they've helped shape, resulting in greater follow-through and ownership.
- Inclusive decisions include diverse viewpoints, experiences, and ideas, which strengthen the vision, enhance relevance, and improve adaptability. This variety enables the group to anticipate challenges and devise innovative solutions.
- Respectful decision-making fosters trust by demonstrating that leadership and group members value everyone's contributions. This cultivates a safe environment where

individuals feel comfortable sharing ideas, concerns, and feedback, all of which are essential for maintaining momentum toward the shared vision.
- Respectful and inclusive decision-making cultivates a sense of belonging, reinforcing that "we're in this together." This enhances group cohesion and encourages cooperative behavior, which is essential for achieving complex, long-term visions.
- Inclusive decision-making encourages continuous feedback, enabling the collective vision to evolve and remain relevant. Respectful engagement motivates individuals to voice their concerns when changes are necessary, helping the group stay on course.

When people see that their input is taken seriously, they feel valued and more committed to shared goals. This can enhance trust in leadership and peers, as everyone feels they are treated fairly. In practical terms, teams that engage in inclusive discussions often make decisions more efficiently and with greater buy-in, as potential objections are addressed upfront. Additionally, drawing on diverse perspectives leads to more creative and robust solutions in the short run, since ideas are evaluated from multiple angles rather than a narrow viewpoint. When decisions are made inclusively and respectfully, the positive impacts range from emotional (trust, confidence, sense of belonging) to tangible performance outcomes (better decisions, effective implementation). While the specifics may vary, the core principle holds across workplaces, schools, community organizations, and families: listening to diverse voices and handling disagreements with respect leads to wiser decisions and stronger, happier groups in the long run.

Chapter 12

Myths and Misunderstandings about Inclusive and Respectful Decision-Making

Several myths and misunderstandings can hinder inclusive and respectful decision-making. Here are some common misconceptions.

Myth/ Misunderstanding	Reality
Inclusion Means Treating Everyone the Same	True inclusion recognizes and values individual differences. Treating everyone identically can overlook unique needs and experiences, whereas equitable practices tailor support to ensure all individuals can participate fully.
Inclusion Is a One-Time Initiative	Inclusion and respect require continuous effort, reflection, and adaptation to meet the evolving needs of individuals and communities.
Respect Requires Agreeing with Everyone	Respect involves acknowledging and valuing others' perspectives, even when there is disagreement. Engaging in open, honest dialogue and considering diverse viewpoints demonstrates respect more than mere agreement.
Respect Is Earned, Not Given	While actions can enhance respect, a foundational level of respect should be extended to all individuals by default. This approach fosters trust and openness, creating a conducive environment for collaborative decision-making.
Being Respectful Means Avoiding Difficult Decisions	Respect doesn't equate to avoiding tough choices or critical feedback. Making difficult decisions and delivering constructive feedback respectfully are essential aspects of leadership and effective decision-making.

Strategies for Fostering Inclusive and Respectful Decision-making

While inclusive and respectful decision-making is gaining traction globally, its prevalence varies across societies and cultures. Factors influencing these practices include cultural norms, gender roles, and socioeconomic conditions. For example, in some regions, traditional patriarchal structures may restrict inclusive decision-making, whereas other societies are progressing towards more egalitarian family dynamics. Although research findings support multiple benefits, many organizations and groups have yet to shift their cultures toward inclusive and respectful decision-making. Some groups and organizations are moving away from inclusive and respectful decision-making by adopting authoritarian or top-down approaches. The following strategies can help transform the culture into one that fosters inclusive and respectful decision-making.

- **Clarify Decision-Making Roles:** Clearly define who is responsible for making decisions and how input from various stakeholders will be considered and incorporated.
- **Document and Share Processes:** Maintain transparency by documenting decision-making procedures and sharing them with all relevant parties.
- **Implement Checks and Balances:** Incorporate mechanisms to prevent biases and ensure accountability throughout the decision-making process.
- **Encourage Diverse Contributions:** Take turns and actively invite input from individuals with diverse backgrounds and experiences to enrich the decision-making process.
- **Balance Interests:** Strive to consider and balance the interests of all stakeholders, especially those from underrepresented groups.

- **Avoid Majority Rule Pitfalls:** Recognize that majority opinions are not always indicative of the best outcomes; value minority perspectives equally.

In Summary

Making decisions in inclusive and respectful ways involves actively engaging diverse voices in the decision-making process, ensuring that all participants feel heard, valued, and empowered to contribute their ideas. This approach emphasizes open communication, empathy, and mutual respect, creating an environment where individuals from varied backgrounds can collaborate effectively.

In the context of a shared vision, inclusive and respectful decision-making fosters a sense of ownership and commitment among team members, as they see their perspectives influencing outcomes. This collective engagement enhances trust, reduces misunderstandings, and leads to more innovative and effective solutions.

Organizations can foster inclusive and respectful decision-making by encouraging open communication, soliciting diverse input, providing training in collaborative problem-solving, creating structured frameworks for gathering feedback, and celebrating successful inclusive decisions.

Chapter 13
We Cooperate

BEING COOPERATIVE MEANS working with others toward a common goal and responding positively to requests for assistance. It requires a willingness to collaborate, communicate effectively, and contribute to group efforts. In the workplace, being cooperative often involves collaborating with colleagues on projects, sharing information, and supporting team decisions. In everyday life, it could entail helping a friend move, participating in community activities, or simply listening and responding constructively in conversations.

In contrast, non-cooperation refers to not working together with someone or not complying with their requests. When people do not cooperate, it indicates a refusal or failure to work together toward a common goal or to follow through on requests. It also represents a breakdown of mutual support and relationships.

While cooperation is generally beneficial, excessive cooperation can be harmful. An overemphasis on harmony and collaboration may sometimes stifle dissenting opinions or critical thinking. When people over-cooperate, they may rely too heavily on the group, resulting in a loss of personal initiative and an increased dependence on the group.

Implications for a Shared Vision

Cooperation is essential for achieving a shared vision because a vision is almost always something larger than what any individual can accomplish alone. Here's why cooperation plays such a critical role:

- A shared vision provides direction, but cooperation ensures that everyone is working together to achieve that vision.
- Without cooperation, people may pursue conflicting agendas, causing fragmentation and inefficiency.
- Collaboration enables individuals to combine their varied talents and utilize their shared strengths, making the vision achievable.
- Cooperation builds trust, mutual respect, and engagement, which are essential for sustained effort toward a long-term vision.
- When people perceive that others are contributing, they are more likely to remain engaged and committed.
- A shared vision often requires continuous dialogue, feedback, and flexibility, all of which are facilitated by cooperation.

Myths and Misunderstandings about Cooperation

Several myths and misunderstandings can hinder inclusive and respectful decision-making. Here are some common misconceptions.

Myth/ Misunderstanding	Reality
Cooperation means no conflict.	Healthy cooperation embraces constructive conflict as a means to surface different ideas, challenge assumptions, and enhance decision-making. A cooperative culture emphasizes resolving disputes respectfully, rather than avoiding them.
Cooperation means that everyone must agree (there is a consensus).	Cooperative cultures emphasize collaboration, mutual respect, and shared goals, but they don't require unanimous agreement on every issue. Decisions can be made through various methods (e.g., majority vote, leadership direction) as long as the process is inclusive and transparent.
Cooperation makes people weak or dependent.	Cooperation strengthens individuals and groups by combining talents and resources. If used correctly, and not to excess, cooperation promotes interdependence, not dependence, meaning people work together while still maintaining their strengths and responsibilities.
Cooperative cultures lack competition or ambition.	Cooperative cultures can still foster personal ambition and performance excellence, but they frame success in terms of collective achievement. Cooperation doesn't suppress achievement; it channels it toward shared success rather than individual gain at the expense of others.

Chapter 13

Myth/ Misunderstanding	Reality
Cooperation slows down decision-making.	While cooperation requires communication and coordination, it streamlines implementation because people are working in alignment with one another. Cooperative decisions may take longer up front, but often lead to faster execution, fewer mistakes, and greater buy-in.
Cooperation happens naturally.	Cooperation needs to be intentionally cultivated through shared values, clear communication, trust-building, and supportive norms. Without deliberate effort, competition, mistrust, or silos may dominate.
Cooperation is only for "nice" people or small groups.	Cooperation can thrive in large organizations or competitive industries if the structures, leadership, and incentives support it. It's a skill and a culture that can be built and sustained across different contexts.
Cooperation eliminates hierarchy or leadership.	Leadership is crucial in cooperative cultures but takes the form of facilitation, empowerment, and support rather than control. Hierarchies may exist, but power is used to enable collaboration, not suppress it.
Cooperation equals uniformity.	True cooperation welcomes diversity of thought and approaches. It's about finding ways to work together despite differences, not erasing them. Diverse perspectives often strengthen cooperative efforts.

Strategies for Fostering Cooperation

Supporting cooperation within a culture requires intentional strategies that build trust, align objectives, and establish systems that encourage collaboration. Here are strategies for fostering cooperation across different settings:

- Acknowledge and celebrate collaborative achievements.
- Create shared rewards—such as team bonuses and group recognition—that hinge on collective success rather than individual performance.
- Develop collaborative workflows by utilizing shared digital tools and joint projects.
- Offer training sessions on collaborative skills.
- Offer team-building activities that emphasize teamwork and cooperation.
- Leaders demonstrate collaboration, openness, and respect in their actions.
- Highlight stories of cooperation and celebrate role models within the group.
- Establish peer mentoring or buddy systems.
- Encourage knowledge sharing and mutual aid within the group.
- Develop rituals that emphasize collective effort, such as shared meals or team celebrations.
- Utilize collaborative platforms such as Slack and Microsoft Teams.
- Include remote and hybrid workers in cooperative activities.
- During performance reviews, conduct surveys on team dynamics.
- During performance reviews, reflect on the successes and challenges of collaboration.

In Summary

Cooperation involves working together towards common goals with mutual support, communication, and trust. It combines diverse talents and perspectives for better problem-solving and innovation. To encourage cooperation, promote open communication, and foster team-building activities, recognize collaboration, and establish clear, shared objectives.

Chapter 14
We Share Responsibility for Making Things Work

SHARING RESPONSIBILITY FOR making things work means that all members of a group, team, organization, household, or community actively contribute to the success and smooth functioning of the collective effort. It involves a mutual commitment in which each person takes ownership not only of their tasks but also of the well-being and effectiveness of the group as a whole. Typically, it includes:

- **Ownership of Outcomes:** People feel accountable not only for their role but also for the success of the entire group or project. This includes stepping up when challenges arise, even if they fall outside one's specific duties.
- **Mutual Support:** Members assist one another to ensure tasks are completed effectively. If someone is struggling, others offer help, advice, or resources to support them.
- **Collective Problem-Solving:** Instead of blaming individuals when things go wrong, the group collaborates to find

solutions. There is a focus on "How do we fix this together?" rather than "Who is at fault?"
- **Open Communication:** There's ongoing, clear, and respectful dialogue about what is needed to succeed. People voice concerns, share ideas, and ask for help when necessary.
- **Adaptability:** Members are willing to adjust their roles or pitch in outside their usual scope when the situation calls for it. Flexibility is a key component of the shared commitment.
- **Shared Vision and Goals:** Everyone understands and aligns with the broader purpose or objectives. This shared sense of direction fuels cooperation and collective action, fostering a unified approach.
- **Trust and Dependability:** Trust is built when people reliably fulfill their commitments and believe others will do the same, thereby strengthening the sense of shared responsibility.

Implications for a Shared Vision

Sharing responsibility plays a crucial role in supporting a shared vision, as it translates abstract ideals into collective action. A shared vision defines where a group wants to go, but sharing responsibility is how they get there, together. Here's how the two connect:

Transform Vision into Action

- A shared vision provides direction and purpose, but without shared responsibility, it risks staying theoretical.
- When people share responsibility, they commit to making the vision real. Everyone asks: "What can I do to move us closer to this?"

Build Ownership and Buy-In

- When people feel responsible for outcomes, they are more emotionally invested in the vision.
- Instead of being passive followers of a leader's vision, they become co-creators of the future.
- This creates intrinsic motivation—people work toward the vision because they believe in it and feel it's theirs.

Enhance Collaboration and Alignment
- A shared vision provides everyone with a common goal to align around, while sharing responsibility ensures collaboration toward achieving that goal.
- It reduces silos or "that's not my job" attitudes because people understand the bigger picture and support one another across roles and boundaries.

Encourage Problem-Solving and Adaptability
- Achieving a shared vision often involves navigating challenges. Sharing responsibility fosters a culture of collective problem-solving.
- When setbacks occur, people step up—not just to protect their interests, but to keep the vision alive.

Foster Trust and Commitment
- Shared responsibility reinforces trust within the group because people see that everyone is doing their part.
- This trust strengthens the commitment to the shared vision, as people feel they are part of a reliable and united effort.

Sustain Momentum Over Time

- Visions take time to achieve. Shared responsibility ensures that no one person carries the full burden, which helps prevent burnout and maintains energy over the long haul.

When people do not share responsibility, it means that individuals avoid taking ownership of the group's success, well-being, or outcomes. Instead of working together to ensure functionality, individuals focus solely on their narrow roles, or worse, they disengage entirely. Consequently, the group's shared goals, including any common vision, tend to suffer.

Myths and Misunderstandings about Sharing Responsibility

Several myths and misunderstandings can hinder people's ability to fully embrace shared responsibility. These misconceptions can discourage collaboration, lower engagement, and prevent groups from functioning at their best.

Myth/Misunderstanding	Reality
Sharing responsibility means no one is truly accountable.	Sharing responsibility means broadening ownership, not diffusing accountability. Each individual is responsible for their contributions as well as promoting the collective achievement of the group. In well-functioning groups, roles and responsibilities are clear, but everyone remains attentive to the group's broader goals.

Myth/Misunderstanding	Reality
If I do my job, that's enough.	Focusing solely on your tasks may mean ignoring the bigger picture. Shared responsibility asks people to consider, "How is my work impacting the team or project as a whole?" It encourages collaboration and support across roles, especially when problems arise or group goals are at stake.
Leaders are solely responsible for outcomes.	While leaders guide and support, success ultimately depends on the contributions of everyone. Over-relying on leadership can create passivity among team members, leading to disengagement and burnout for both leaders and team members. Effective teams see every member as a stakeholder in achieving the vision.
If responsibility is shared, people will slack off.	This assumes people won't step up without strict oversight, but in healthy cultures, shared responsibility fosters trust and motivation. When people feel a sense of ownership, they're often more committed and proactive because they know their contributions matter.
Sharing responsibility leads to chaos and confusion.	This can happen when clear communication and defined roles are absent. But true shared responsibility combines clarity with collaboration. People are aware of their specific duties but also empowered to support one another and address challenges as they arise.

Chapter 14

Myth/Misunderstanding	Reality
Only certain people are capable or qualified to take responsibility.	Everyone has something valuable to contribute, even if it's asking questions, offering feedback, or supporting others. Shared responsibility builds capacity in the group, encouraging growth and skill-sharing rather than limiting contributions to a select few.
If I share responsibility, I'll have to do more work.	Sharing responsibility involves collaborating to improve efficiency, rather than increasing the number of tasks. Often, it reduces individual burdens because problems are solved collaboratively rather than left to one person.
Shared responsibility is only for formal teams or organizations.	Families, communities, and social groups all benefit from shared responsibility. Whether it's planning an event, caring for a household, or contributing to a neighborhood project, shared ownership fosters stronger connections and greater success in any setting.

Strategies for Improving Shared Responsibility in a Subculture

Improving shared responsibility within a subculture—whether it's a workplace team, family, or community group—requires intentional actions that build trust, clarity, ownership, and a sense of belonging. The goal is to create an environment where people feel motivated and empowered to contribute not only to their roles but also to the collective success of the group. Here's a breakdown of strategies to foster and strengthen shared responsibility:

Clarify the Shared Vision and Goals
- Ensure that everyone understands the broader context—why the group exists and what it aims to achieve.
- Reinforce how each person's contribution supports the vision.
- Use visuals, stories, or shared language to keep the vision alive.

Define Roles and Expectations Clearly—But Flexibly
- Outline who is responsible for what, but emphasize that everyone supports the whole.
- Encourage a "see something, say something, do something" mindset—if someone notices an issue, they feel empowered to act or bring it forward, even if it's outside their formal role.

Promote Mutual Accountability
- Utilize team check-ins, peer feedback, or progress reviews where group members, not just leaders, hold one another accountable.
- Celebrate shared wins and discuss setbacks together, focusing on how the group can improve.

Encourage Collaboration and Cross-Role Support
- Create opportunities for collaboration across roles or departments.
- Rotate leadership or coordination roles on projects to spread ownership.

Leaders Model Responsibility
- Leaders should model vulnerability and openness by admitting when they need help, inviting feedback, and participating alongside the group.
- Leaders can ask questions like, "What support do we need as a group to meet this goal?" and, "How can we help each other be successful?"

Recognize and Celebrate Contributions
- Regularly acknowledge group efforts and individual contributions that support the collective.
- Frame recognition around shared responsibility with messages such as "Thanks to everyone who stepped up to make this happen."

Foster Psychological Safety
- Ensure the group is a safe space to take risks, admit mistakes, and ask for help.
- Shared responsibility flourishes when trust is present.

Use Storytelling and Narratives
- Share stories of when the group succeeded together, emphasizing collective action.
- Narratives help reinforce the identity of the subculture as one where everyone contributes. For example, "Remember when we all pulled together to meet that tight deadline? That's what makes this team strong."

Measure and Reflect Together

Periodically reflect as a group with questions such as, "How well are we sharing responsibility?" and "What can we improve?"

In Summary

A subculture that supports sharing responsibility for achieving success is characterized by a collaborative approach, where members of a group actively contribute to the achievement of shared goals. Rather than relying solely on designated leaders or specific roles, this principle encourages everyone to take initiative, offer support, and be accountable for outcomes. In the context of a shared vision, distributing responsibility fosters a sense of ownership and commitment among team members, enhancing motivation and cohesion. To cultivate a subculture that supports shared responsibility, organizations can promote open communication, establish clear expectations, and recognize contributions from all levels. Encouraging participatory decision-making and providing opportunities for skill development further empower individuals to take on responsibilities, leading to a more resilient and adaptive team dynamic.

Chapter 15

We Have Clear and Consistent Goals

FOR A SUBCULTURE to have clear and consistent goals means that the group shares a well-defined understanding of what everyone is working toward and maintains steady alignment on these objectives over time. These goals are specific enough to guide action, relevant to the group's shared purpose or identity, and consistently reinforced across the subculture's activities, communications, and decisions. Key elements of having clear and consistent goals include:

Clarity:
- Members of the subculture understand what the goals are, why they matter, and *how* members can contribute.
- Goals are communicated in straightforward, accessible language.
- Priorities are unambiguous—there's no confusion about which objectives are most important.

Consistency:
- Goals remain stable over time (although they may evolve), allowing members to build trust and commitment.
- Messages, decisions, and behaviors across the group align with the stated goals—there's little discrepancy between what is said and what is done.
- Reinforcement happens through repeated communication, rituals, role modeling, and recognition of goal-aligned behavior.

Alignment with Subculture Identity:
- Goals reflect the values, norms, and mission of the subculture, fostering shared direction and a sense of belonging that connects members through collective efforts.

Guidance for Action:
- Clear goals help members make day-to-day decisions and prioritize their activities.
- Goals foster accountability—people know what success looks like and can measure progress.

Here are examples of clear and consistent goals that support shared values and foster collective well-being across households, groups, and communities:

- **A Goal for Fostering Open Communication in a Household:** Hold a family meeting every Sunday evening to discuss schedules, challenges, and successes.
- **A Goal for Promoting Health and Wellness in a Household:** Prepare and share at least five home-cooked meals each week with nutritious ingredients.

- **A Goal for Financial Responsibility in a Household:** Save 10% of household income monthly toward a shared vacation or emergency fund.
- **A Goal for Enhancing Team Collaboration in a Workgroup:** Implement biweekly check-in meetings to review progress, address concerns, and share successes.
- **A Goal for Professional Development in a Workgroup:** Ensure that every team member attends at least one skill-building workshop per quarter.
- **A Goal for Customer Service Excellence in a Workgroup:** Achieve and maintain a customer satisfaction score of 90% or higher each quarter.
- **A Goal for Building Social Connections in a Community:** Host monthly community events (e.g., potlucks, workshops, clean-up days) to encourage engagement and connection.
- **A Goal for Civic Engagement in the Community:** Register at least 500 new voters in the community before the next election cycle.
- **A Goal for Environmental Stewardship in the Community:** Reduce community waste by 25% over the next year through targeted recycling initiatives and educational campaigns.

Implications for a Shared Vision

Having clear and consistent goals is one of the most practical ways to support, reinforce, and operationalize a shared vision within a subculture. While a shared vision provides the big-picture purpose or aspirational direction, clear and consistent goals break that vision down into actionable steps that guide daily behaviors, decisions, and priorities.

Chapter 15

Myths and Misunderstandings about Sharing Responsibility

There are several myths and misunderstandings about having clear and consistent goals that can prevent subcultures from setting or maintaining effective direction.

Myth/ Misunderstanding	Reality
Goals limit creativity and flexibility.	Clear goals provide structure but don't dictate how to achieve them. They offer a framework that can enhance creativity by focusing efforts while allowing flexibility in methods. Well-crafted goals can even stimulate innovation by encouraging members to find new solutions to achieve shared outcomes.
Everyone already knows the goals, so they don't need to be stated.	When goals aren't stated explicitly, there's room for misinterpretation or misalignment. Regularly articulating and reinforcing goals ensures shared understanding and keeps everyone aligned, especially as circumstances evolve.
Once goals are set, they should never change.	Goals should be consistent with the vision but adaptable to new information, challenges, or opportunities. Flexibility in strategies, while staying anchored to the shared vision, helps keep goals relevant and practical.
More goals = better results.	Too many goals can dilute focus and overwhelm members, leading to burnout or underperformance. Fewer, well-prioritized goals are more effective, as they provide clarity and focus on what matters most.
Goals are only for leaders or managers.	The best goals are co-created and shared among all members of the subculture. Involvement fosters ownership, engagement, and alignment, making it more likely that goals will be embraced and pursued.

Myth/ Misunderstanding	Reality
Having goals guarantees success.	Goals require consistent communication, adequate resources, accountability, and flexibility to adapt effectively. Success also depends on buy-in, collaboration, and ongoing reinforcement.
Goals are only about metrics and numbers.	While quantitative goals are helpful, qualitative goals, such as improving trust or collaboration, are equally important. Qualitative goals can be supported by observations, feedback, or narratives, even if they aren't easily quantified.
Once agreed upon, goals don't need to be discussed again.	Regular check-ins ensure that goals stay top-of-mind, remain relevant, and can be adapted as needed. Revisiting goals reinforces commitment and allows adjustments based on progress or changing circumstances.
Goals are only for workplaces, not families or communities.	Households, friend groups, and communities also benefit from clear goals. Shared goals strengthen relationships, trust, and collective action across all types of subcultures.

Strategies for Having Clear and Consistent Goals Within a Subculture

Setting clear and consistent goals in a subculture requires thoughtful collaboration, alignment with shared values, and ongoing communication. The process should foster ownership, engagement, and adaptability while anchoring the group to its shared vision:

1. **Start with the Shared Vision and Values**
   - Ensure alignment: Goals should support the bigger picture—the group's shared vision and core values.
   - Ask reflective questions to ensure the goals feel meaningful and connected to the subculture's identity:
     - "What do we stand for as a group?"
     - "What future are we trying to create together?"

2. **Involve Members in Goal-Setting**
   - Collaborate: Engage the group in co-creating goals through discussions, surveys, or workshops, fostering buy-in and shared ownership.
   - Incorporate diverse perspectives: Encourage input from different members to ensure goals reflect the needs, insights, and priorities of the whole group.

3. **Include Both Qualitative and Quantitative Goals**
   - Quantitative goals are measurable and time-bound (with deadlines and review points).
   - Qualitative goals clarify the overall intention.

4. **Prioritize Goals to Maintain Focus**
   - Limit the number of goals: Focus on a few high-priority objectives to prevent overwhelm and dilution of effort.

5. **Define Roles and Responsibilities**
   - Clarify who does what: Assign clear responsibilities to individuals or teams for achieving each goal. This prevents confusion and ensures accountability while promoting shared contributions.

6. Communicate Goals Clearly and Frequently
- Reinforce goals through regular communication (e.g., in meetings, newsletters, visual reminders).
- Use multiple formats—written, verbal, and visual—to ensure that the communication resonates with the subculture.
- Reiterate why the goals matter and how they align with the shared vision.

7. Integrate Goals into Daily Practices
- Embed goals into routines, decision-making processes, and cultural rituals.
- Start team meetings by regularly reviewing progress toward goals or celebrating small wins.

8. Create Feedback Loops and Checkpoints
- Schedule regular reviews to assess progress, reflect on progress, and adjust goals as needed.
- Utilize feedback loops from group members to understand both barriers and successes, ensuring the goals remain relevant.

9. Celebrate Progress and Successes
- Recognize milestones and achievements, no matter how small. This reinforces motivation, builds momentum, and strengthens the subculture's sense of shared accomplishment.

10. Adapt When Necessary, While Staying Anchored to the Vision
- Be willing to adjust goals in response to changing circumstances without losing sight of the overarching vision.

- Encourage flexibility in methods, while maintaining consistency in purpose.

In Summary

Having clear and consistent goals means establishing specific, well-defined objectives that are uniformly understood and pursued by all members of a team or organization. These goals serve as a roadmap, guiding collective efforts and ensuring that everyone is aligned in their actions and decisions.

In the context of a shared vision, clear and consistent goals are crucial because they provide direction and purpose, enabling team members to coordinate effectively and work toward common outcomes. Without such clarity, efforts may become fragmented, leading to confusion and inefficiency. A shared vision, supported by well-articulated goals, fosters unity and enhances the team's ability to achieve its objectives.

To create a supportive subculture, establish and communicate clear goals that align with values, engage everyone in setting these goals, provide regular feedback and recognition, and adjust goals as necessary.

Chapter 16

We Are Free to Do Things

IN SUBCULTURES THAT support freedom, individuals have autonomy in their approach to tasks and responsibilities. In such subcultures, people are trusted to utilize their strengths and styles to achieve their objectives, and groups have the freedom to pursue their goals in a manner they deem appropriate. Here are examples of how households, workplaces, and communities can support freedom in decision-making:

In Households
- Members of a household can make collaborative decisions on charitable donations and major purchases, promoting mutual respect and shared responsibility.
- Parents may allow children to choose extracurricular activities or manage personal budgets, helping them develop decision-making skills and confidence.

In Workplaces
- Companies may grant employees full autonomy over when and where they work, focusing on outcomes rather than processes.
- Some workplaces implement innovation days, allowing employees to work on any project of their choice, fostering creativity and ownership.
- Companies often have employee suggestion boxes, allowing staff to propose ideas and improvements, which can lead to tangible changes and increased engagement.

In Communities
- Cities and towns may involve residents in allocating portions of the municipal budget, ensuring community needs and preferences are directly addressed.
- Communities can engage local stakeholders in developing and implementing local initiatives, ensuring that decisions reflect the collective vision and needs of the community.
- Establishing town hall meetings or online platforms where community members can voice opinions and influence decisions on local matters can promote transparency and trust.

Providing individuals and groups with the freedom to operate in their own way is about creating a supportive environment where autonomy and alignment coexist; it is not about relinquishing all control. This balance empowers teams to take initiative, fosters innovation, and strengthens commitment to the shared vision, ultimately driving organizational success.

Implications for a Shared Vision

Supporting freedom plays a pivotal role in fostering a shared vision within teams and organizations. When people are empowered to make decisions and approach tasks in ways that align with their strengths and perspectives, they develop a more profound sense of ownership over their work. This personal investment translates into a more substantial commitment to the organization's overarching goals. When accountability coexists with autonomy, teams work collaboratively, think creatively, and push boundaries, all while staying aligned with the organization's purpose.

Autonomy enables individuals to align their personal goals with the organization's vision, which is crucial for achieving shared objectives and sustaining collective momentum. In addition, people are more likely to seek out new knowledge and skills when they have the freedom to explore and innovate. This adaptability is crucial for organizations seeking to evolve and remain aligned with their shared vision in a rapidly changing environment.

Myths and Misunderstandings about Sharing Responsibility

There are several myths and misunderstandings surrounding the relationship between freedom and autonomy and a shared vision.

Myth/ Misunderstanding	Reality
Freedom means a lack of structure.	Giving people freedom doesn't mean abandoning structure or goals. Instead, it means providing clear expectations for outcomes while allowing flexibility in how those outcomes are achieved. Freedom works best when paired with clarity about shared vision, goals, and values.

Chapter 16

Myth/ Misunderstanding	Reality
People will become lazy or unmotivated if given freedom.	Research has found that autonomy tends to increase motivation, creativity, and accountability. When people feel trusted and respected, they are more likely to invest themselves fully in their tasks.
Everyone wants complete freedom.	While autonomy is important, most people also want support, feedback, and guidance. Excessive freedom without support can lead to anxiety, confusion, or feelings of isolation. A healthy balance between freedom and connection to the group is crucial.
Freedom will lead to chaos or disorganization.	Chaos usually results from unclear goals, poor communication, or a lack of trust, rather than from autonomy itself. If people understand the shared vision and standards, freedom can support coordination because individuals can adapt fluidly while staying aligned.
Only highly skilled or senior people can handle freedom.	Even less experienced individuals can thrive when given freedom that is scaled to their level of development. Freedom can—and should—grow over time through mentorship, coaching, and practice.
Freedom undermines leadership authority.	Effective leadership is not about control; it's about empowerment. Leaders who give their people freedom are respected because they trust and develop them, rather than issuing orders. Shared decision-making can strengthen leadership credibility.
Freedom means everyone must work alone.	Freedom can exist alongside collaboration. People can choose how to work together, set norms, and self-organize in ways that maximize their talents while still supporting team efforts.

Strategies for Creating Subcultures that Give People the Freedom to Do Things Their Way

Freedom and autonomy thrive best when embedded intentionally into a culture's norms, systems, and expectations. The culture can encourage independence and set boundaries that let people know that they have a degree of freedom. Here's how you can systematically increase cultural support for autonomy across households, workplaces, and communities:

- Create a shared vision that focuses on *what* needs to be achieved, not how.
- Regularly revisit the vision to keep people aligned while allowing personal initiative.
- Leaders and influential members should demonstrate that they trust others to make decisions.
- Publicly recognize stories where individuals or teams succeeded by exercising autonomy. Such stories will inspire and show that freedom to innovate is not just acceptable but also celebrated.
- Encourage respectful debate and experimentation.
- Normalize feedback loops where adjustments are made without shaming.
- Let people choose their methods, timelines, and roles when appropriate.
- Offer options even in small areas (e.g., meeting times, project styles).
- Provide coaching, mentoring, or workshops on decision-making, risk assessment, and self-management.
- Gradually expand people's decision-making authority as they gain confidence.

- Define clear boundaries (e.g., ethical standards, budget limits). Within those guardrails, encourage freedom and creativity.
- Encourage ownership, not just compliance, by designating meaningful responsibilities. Frame tasks as contributions to the broader picture, rather than just assignments.
- Allow teams to self-organize, select leaders, and distribute tasks.
- Encourage peer accountability rather than top-down enforcement.
- Repeatedly state that initiative and ownership are valued.
- Ask, "What do you need to succeed?" rather than "Why did you do it that way?"
- Build indicators of autonomy and ownership into evaluations and celebrations.
- Reward innovation, self-starting, and collaborative leadership.

In Summary

A subculture that supports freedom for people to do things their way encourages individuals to make choices and act in ways that align with their styles, strengths, and insights. This type of freedom fosters innovation, personal investment, and a sense of ownership, which are essential for sustaining motivation and engagement. In the context of a shared vision, allowing freedom helps people connect their unique contributions to the group's broader goals, enhancing both creativity and commitment. Subcultures that support this kind of freedom cultivate trust and clearly define shared goals while allowing flexibility in methods.

These subcultures also encourage open communication and mutual respect. Strategies for creating such a subculture include promoting psychological safety, reducing micromanagement, celebrating diverse approaches, and empowering individuals to take initiative and learn from experience.

PART III
FOSTERING A POSITIVE OUTLOOK

THERE ARE SIMILARITIES between individual optimism and a positive outlook within a culture. Individuals can enjoy an upbeat and optimistic outlook. In a similar manner, a subculture with a positive outlook will have norms that promote enthusiasm, hope, effective conflict resolution, and high standards. In a subculture with a positive outlook, individuals feel valued, supported, and motivated to contribute to shared goals. Subcultures characterized by a positive outlook encourage optimism, resilience, and constructive thinking. There are expectations for favorable outcomes, viewing setbacks as temporary and manageable while maintaining confidence in one's ability to cope and grow. In these subcultures, there is a tendency to recognize possibilities, solutions, and hopeful expectations, even in the face of challenges. A positive outlook encompasses a range of attitudes and behaviors. Where a positive outlook exists, there is strong consensus that:

- We maintain high standards for how we function.
- We have a high level of team spirit.
- We resolve conflicts in positive ways.
- We celebrate achievements.
- We have a can-do attitude.
- We are proud of our group.

Each of these attitudes and behaviors contributes to a positive outlook. How do your social environments foster and maintain a positive outlook? Don't be discouraged if your group, organization, neighborhood, family, or household lacks one or more of these elements. In the following chapters, we will examine these attitudes and behaviors more closely and explore ways to enhance each of them.

It is surprisingly common for subcultures within organizations, teams, or communities to develop a negative outlook, especially when facing ongoing challenges. In U.S. workplaces, more than a quarter of organizational subunits, such as departments and teams, are estimated to experience low morale, negativity, or resistance to change. Many groups tend to focus on what is going wrong rather than building upon what is working well. A culture with a negative outlook fosters pessimism, distrust, and the belief that improvement is unlikely or impossible. In such cultures—whether in workplaces, communities, or teams—people often expect failure, avoid taking initiative, and feel disempowered.

Groups and Organizations Benefit from a Positive Outlook

A positive outlook within a subculture can serve as a powerful force for enhancing individual well-being, group cohesion, and organizational success. It creates an emotional climate that enables people to thrive rather than just cope. The benefits of a positive outlook for groups and organizations include:

- **Performance and productivity:** A better focus, initiative, and results.
- **Conflict and communication:** Healthier feedback and reduced defensiveness.
- **Adaptability and change readiness:** Faster adjustment to change, more positive framing.
- **Positive influence on other groups:** Modeling spreads optimism across groups.
- **Social bonds:** Improved trust, inclusion, and mutual support.
- **Motivation and engagement:** A greater sense of purpose, energy, and follow-through.
- **Creativity and innovation:** More innovation, flexibility, and idea generation.

Health and Well-being Benefits of a Positive Outlook

A positive outlook provides significant health and well-being benefits, including:

- **Reduced Stress and anxiety:** A positive outlook helps lower cortisol levels and enables individuals to recover from stress more quickly. Optimistic people perceive challenges as manageable, reducing the psychological burden.
- **Greater resilience:** A positive mindset supports "bounce-back" ability after adversity, trauma, or illness. It is linked to better coping strategies such as active problem-solving and reframing.
- **Lower risk of depression:** Positive emotions counteract rumination and helplessness, reducing depression symptoms. A positive outlook encourages social support and engagement, which are protective factors against mental health challenges.
- **Improved self-esteem and purpose:** Optimism fosters a stronger belief in personal agency and self-worth. People with a positive outlook often report a stronger sense of meaning and life satisfaction.
- **Greater emotional regulation:** Optimists tend to be better at managing fear, anger, and sadness. A positive outlook promotes acceptance, gratitude, and mindfulness.
- **Lower risk of cardiovascular disease:** Researchers are discovering a connection between optimism and improved heart health, lower blood pressure, and reduced inflammation.
- **Stronger immune function:** A positive outlook boosts immune responses, making individuals more resistant to illness. This phenomenon has been observed in response to vaccines and common viruses.

- **Faster recovery from illness and surgery:** Optimistic patients heal faster and experience fewer complications. They're also more likely to follow medical advice and engage in healthy behaviors.
- **Longevity:** Research from Harvard and other institutions has found that optimism is associated with a longer lifespan, particularly in women.

Myths and Misunderstandings about Positive Outlook

There are numerous myths and misunderstandings about a positive outlook that can distort its meaning and undermine efforts to enhance it. Here are several of the more harmful myths and misunderstandings:

Myths and Misunderstandings about Positive Outlook

Myth/ Misunderstanding	Reality
Subcultures are not positive or negative. This is about individuals.	Both groups and individuals can have positive or negative outlooks. In a negative subculture, individual and group negativity are accepted and expected.
Having a positive outlook means ignoring problems.	Having a true positive outlook means acknowledging problems and believing that it's possible to respond constructively to them. It's about realistic optimism, not denial.
Positive subcultures are always cheerful and conflict-free.	Genuine positivity includes healthy conflict, constructive feedback, and space for hard conversations. A positive subculture promotes psychological safety, not forced harmony.

Myth/ Misunderstanding	Reality
A positive outlook is naive or unrealistic.	Being positive doesn't mean ignoring reality. Many highly effective leaders and problem-solvers maintain a positive outlook while remaining grounded in facts.
Culture change is only top-down.	While leadership matters, positive subcultures often begin with grassroots efforts or emerge within pockets of larger, less supportive systems.
Positive cultures are soft and unproductive.	Positive subcultures often have higher performance, innovation, and engagement because people feel safe, valued, and motivated.
A subculture can remain positive regardless of the larger system.	Positive subcultures can survive in harsh environments, but they require supportive boundaries, leadership protection, and external allies to thrive in the long term.

Books about a Positive Outlook

The following books offer valuable guidance and research on cultivating a positive outlook:

The Happiness Advantage, by Shawn Achor, demonstrates how positivity fuels success and outlines practical steps for embedding optimism in organizational cultures.

Learned Optimism, by Martin Seligman, demonstrates how optimism can be cultivated, particularly in challenging environments.

Positive Psychology at Work, by Sarah Lewis, provides practical insights into how teams and organizations can cultivate cultures that promote psychological well-being and resilience.

An Everyone Culture: Becoming a Deliberately Developmental Organization, by Robert Kegan and Lisa Lahey, explores how organizations can build growth-minded cultures where psychological safety and optimism are integral to the system.

Culture Renovation, by Kevin Oakes, is a practical guide for transforming workplace culture while preserving what works, with a focus on long-term positivity.

Crucial Conversations, by Kerry Patterson et al., teaches how open and respectful communication can transform conflict-prone cultures into positive, solution-focused environments.

Chapter 17

We Maintain High Standards

Having high standards means that a group, team, household, or community consistently expects and strives for excellence in how people interact, collaborate, and fulfill their responsibilities. It reflects a shared commitment to doing things well, not just achieving outcomes, but also maintaining integrity, respect, accountability, and care throughout the process.

In such subcultures, there is a clear and consistent belief that individuals and groups can achieve high-quality performance, and that they should strive to meet those high standards in their work, behavior, and interactions. People understand what "excellent" looks like in specific contexts, such as thoughtful communication, thorough work, and ethical behavior. Mistakes are viewed as learning opportunities, while shortcuts and complacency are discouraged. People are motivated and challenged to reach their potential, not pressured or shamed. Excellence is the standard, not the exception, and it applies to everyone, including leaders. It's about fostering a subculture where people are encouraged and supported to do their best, learn continuously, and take pride in what they do.

Maintaining high standards promotes a positive outlook by cultivating a culture of hope, pride, and confidence in what is achievable. When people are encouraged to strive for excellence and hold themselves and others accountable in constructive ways, it conveys a powerful message: "We believe in each other's potential and the value of doing things well."

Implications for a Positive Outlook

High standards foster an environment in which individuals expect positive outcomes for themselves, one another, and the future—essential elements of a positive outlook. High standards can:

- **Promote a Sense of Purpose:** High standards give people meaningful goals to work toward, creating a sense that their efforts matter and contribute to something worthwhile.
- **Build Confidence and Optimism:** Achieving high standards reinforces the belief that success is attainable. This helps foster individual and group confidence, leading to greater optimism about the future.
- **Encourage a Growth Mindset:** High standards assume that people can improve and learn. This fosters resilience and a belief that challenges can be overcome.
- **Foster Pride and Motivation:** When people meet or exceed high standards, it leads to pride in their work and their group, reinforcing positive emotions and motivation.
- **Reduce Tolerance for Negativity and Dysfunction:** High standards make it less likely that toxic behavior, apathy, or poor performance will go unchallenged, fostering a more uplifting and respectful environment.

> **Important Caveat**
>
> High standards must be accompanied by psychological safety, realistic expectations, and support systems. Without these, high standards can lead to pressure, burnout, and negative self-perceptions—undermining the positive outlook they are meant to foster.

When high standards aren't shared, the group's potential is compromised, and the social climate often drifts toward dysfunction instead of growth. Without common standards, expectations differ from person to person, leading to miscommunication, frustration, and inconsistent quality of work or behavior. When some individuals cut corners or exert little effort without being held accountable, others may feel discouraged or resentful. This makes it harder to take pride in belonging to the group. People lose trust in each other's reliability and integrity. Such conditions undermine collaboration, especially when accountability is absent or applied unfairly. Low standards often allow poor behavior or careless work to persist unchecked, creating a culture where individuals disengage or withdraw. A lack of high standards can breed cynicism, apathy, or passive acceptance of the status quo, undermining hope, enthusiasm, and well-being.

Myths and Misunderstandings about Having High Standards

Several myths and misunderstandings can hinder people from having high standards. These misconceptions can discourage collaboration, reduce engagement, and prevent groups from functioning at their best.

Myth/ Misunderstanding	Reality
High standards mean perfection is expected.	High standards encourage individuals to do their best and learn from mistakes, rather than striving for perfection. They support growth, not punishment for imperfection.
High standards create pressure and stress.	When paired with clear expectations, support, and encouragement, high standards foster purpose and pride, rather than toxic stress. The key is how they are communicated and reinforced.
Only leaders or top performers need to meet high standards.	For a culture of excellence to thrive, *everyone* should be included and supported in upholding high standards.
High standards are rigid and inflexible.	Healthy standards adapt to context and capacity, setting clear goals while allowing room for creativity, learning, and progress over time.
High standards can reduce collaboration and foster a competitive environment.	Shared high standards foster mutual respect and teamwork by creating a common foundation for quality and accountability.
People won't rise to high standards.	When people feel supported and trusted, they often rise above expectations. High standards can be inspiring when tied to a belief in others' potential.

Strategies for Fostering a Subculture with High Standards

Fostering a subculture with high standards involves creating a collective commitment to excellence through leadership, modeling, support, and reinforcement. It's not only about setting expectations, but also about cultivating an environment where individuals take pride in how they collaborate and hold one another accountable in respectful and constructive ways. To create a subculture with high expectations:

- Define what excellence looks like in behavior, performance, and relationships.
- Use written guidelines, team norms, or mission statements that reflect high standards.
- Use role modeling to build trust and signal that the standards apply to everyone. Leaders and respected members should consistently exemplify the standards in their actions.
- Involve members in co-creating the standards to increase buy-in and commitment.
- Encourage group discussions about what "doing things well" means in daily practice.
- Acknowledge and celebrate when individuals or teams meet or exceed standards.
- Use praise, awards, or stories that highlight positive examples.
- Normalize giving and receiving feedback in respectful, solution-oriented ways.
- Use feedback as a learning tool, not as a source of blame.
- Offer mentoring, coaching, and training to equip people with the necessary tools to meet expectations.
- Emphasize improvement over perfection.
- Address behavior or performance that falls short of shared standards.
- Have clear, respectful processes for addressing concerns and resolving issues.

- Begin meetings by revisiting shared values or accomplishments.
- Build reflection and accountability into regular check-ins.
- Pair high standards with empathy, encouragement, and a belief in people's potential. This balance fosters a culture of both excellence and well-being.

Summing Up

Having high standards means expecting excellence in how individuals and groups function—how they communicate, collaborate, and carry out responsibilities. It involves a shared commitment to doing things thoughtfully, reliably, and respectfully, with a focus on quality and integrity. High standards support a positive outlook by promoting purpose, pride, and a belief in each other's potential. They build trust, encourage growth, and help groups achieve consistent, meaningful outcomes. When shared, they reduce dysfunction, raise morale, and foster a sense of shared responsibility. Without them, groups often experience confusion, low motivation, and an erosion of trust.

Chapter 18
We Have Team Spirit

A HIGH LEVEL of team spirit indicates that group members share a strong sense of camaraderie, mutual support, and collective enthusiasm for achieving shared goals. It reflects a positive emotional atmosphere where people feel connected, valued, and motivated to contribute to the team's success. Team members experience a bond and unity, focusing on a clear and compelling common goal to which everyone is committed. Members actively help, encourage, and rely on one another. Individuals find satisfaction in being part of the group and celebrate their joint accomplishments. Interactions are respectful, inclusive, and energizing. The team recovers from setbacks with a "we're in this together" mindset.

A strong sense of team spirit is evident when members of a household, workplace, or community feel united, motivated, and dedicated to working collaboratively toward common goals. Here are examples of how this manifests:

Households

- Family members willingly help each other with chores, childcare, and daily routines without resentment or constant reminders.
- Individuals celebrate one another's achievements, comfort each other in times of stress, and foster a warm, inclusive environment.
- Everyone has a voice in family decisions, fostering a sense of ownership and unity.
- Family dinners, game nights, or holiday customs reinforce connection and group identity.

Workplaces

- Colleagues share knowledge, back each other up, and prioritize team success over personal gain.
- Employees display positive energy, take initiative, and speak well of the organization.
- Team members regularly acknowledge and appreciate each other's efforts and contributions.
- Staff are aligned around a common mission or goal and feel proud to be part of the team.

Communities

- Residents participate in neighborhood cleanups, town meetings, or cultural events with a sense of enthusiasm and responsibility.
- Neighbors assist each other—whether it's checking in on elders, organizing meal trains, or sharing resources during emergencies.

- People often express pride in their community through local branding, festivals, or support for local causes.
- Disagreements are addressed respectfully and constructively, with a priority on the well-being of the group.

When there isn't a high level of team spirit, the group often feels disconnected, unmotivated, and disjointed. Individuals may act more like isolated contributors than members of a cohesive team, which leads to tension, inefficiency, and low morale. Team members may be guarded, suspicious, or hesitant to rely on each other. Information isn't shared openly; misunderstandings and misinterpretations occur frequently. People feel indifferent about team goals and display little enthusiasm or initiative. There's a "that's not my job" mentality; individuals don't contribute or extend themselves beyond their tasks. Instead of collaborating to solve problems, team members point fingers or engage in passive-aggressive behavior. Individuals feel excluded, undervalued, or disconnected from the group.

Implications for a Positive Outlook

When a subculture exhibits a strong sense of team spirit, it promotes a positive outlook among its members by nurturing connection, trust, and a shared belief in the group's potential. The emotional energy, connection, and mutual support generated by robust team spirit cultivate a climate of hope, resilience, and enthusiasm about the future. This collective emotional strength helps sustain confidence and optimism, even in the face of setbacks. A high team spirit encourages:

- **Increased Optimism:** When people feel they are part of a united and supportive team, they are more likely to believe

in the group's ability to overcome challenges and achieve its goals.
- **Emotional Uplift:** Positive interactions, humor, encouragement, and celebration of shared successes all contribute to a more joyful and energizing atmosphere.
- **Greater Resilience:** High team spirit provides emotional support. People are less likely to feel isolated during hard times, which helps them recover more quickly and maintain hope.
- **Shared Purpose and Belonging**: Feeling "in it together" boosts morale. People are more motivated and hopeful when they feel connected to something larger than themselves.
- **Reduced Negativity and Cynicism:** When team spirit is high, there is less room for blame, pessimism, or defeatist thinking. Positive peer influence becomes a powerful force for good.
- **Culture of Encouragement: Members of groups** with a high team spirit often reinforce each other's strengths and progress, reinforcing the belief that good outcomes are not only possible but likely.

Myths and Misunderstandings about Having High Team Spirit

There are numerous myths and misunderstandings surrounding what it means for a subculture to possess high team spirit, which can result in unrealistic expectations, mismanagement, or an underestimation of its value. Recognizing these misconceptions helps ensure that team spirit is cultivated in healthy, effective ways.

Myth/ Misunderstanding	Reality
Team spirit means everyone always agrees.	High team spirit includes trust and openness, which make it easier to have honest disagreements. It's not about avoiding conflict but handling it respectfully and constructively.
Team spirit can't exist in high-pressure or competitive environments.	Many high-performing groups—such as surgical teams, military units, or athletic squads—thrive on strong team spirit, even under stress. Support and cohesion are especially valuable in demanding contexts.
It's just about being social or having fun.	Camaraderie can contribute to enjoyable interactions, but true team spirit is defined by a common purpose, mutual support, and commitment, rather than casual conversation or social events.
Team spirit happens naturally if you hire the right people.	While personalities matter, team spirit usually needs to be cultivated through intentional leadership, shared goals, trust-building, and cultural reinforcement.
Strong individual performers don't need team spirit.	Even top performers benefit from a strong, supportive culture. Team spirit enhances communication, resilience, and morale, which in turn improves the performance of everyone, including high achievers.
Too much team spirit leads to groupthink.	Genuine team spirit fosters inclusion and diverse perspectives. Conversely, groupthink tends to arise in teams facing pressure to conform, rather than supporting constructive cohesion.

Strategies for Fostering a Subculture with a High Team Spirit

High team spirit doesn't come from a single initiative. It's the result of consistent, culturally embedded behaviors that foster a sense of belonging, purpose, and emotional connection. Boosting spirit isn't about superficially "cheering people up"—it's about cultivating connection, meaning, and energy in ways that feel authentic, participatory, and emotionally safe. There are various ways to strengthen team spirit:

- Openly recognize that morale is low or that people are struggling.
- Create safe spaces for people to share concerns or frustrations.
- Avoid toxic positivity—acknowledge difficulties and balance empathy with encouragement.
- Personally thank individuals for their effort and care.
- Start meetings with rounds of appreciation or recognition.
- Highlight small wins, unsung heroes, and acts of kindness.
- Remind the group why their work or effort matters.
- Share stories of the group making a difference or overcoming past challenges.
- Reaffirm the mission and celebrate how far the group has come.
- Organize light-hearted events, such as themed days, games, and shared meals.
- Use humor, music, or uplifting videos to energize meetings.
- Celebrate milestones, even small ones, to spark a sense of progress.
- Ask for ideas: "What would help us feel better as a team?"
- Delegate roles in planning uplifting activities or improvement efforts.
- Let the group co-create solutions for moving forward together.
- Set a short-term goal or challenge the group can rally around.

- Break long-term challenges into achievable steps with visible progress.
- Use visuals or metaphors (such as a journey or a rising sun) to reinforce hope.
- Keep everyone informed, even when the news is tough.
- Adopt a tone that is honest, calm, and future-focused.
- Invite feedback and listen actively.
- Share an inspiring video or quote that resonates with the group.
- Ask a respected outsider to offer perspective or encouragement.

Summing Up

Team spirit is the shared sense of camaraderie, trust, and mutual commitment that unites group members in working toward common goals. It embodies a culture of support, pride, and emotional connection, where individuals feel valued, interconnected, and motivated to contribute. Team spirit is essential because it boosts morale, enhances collaboration, increases resilience, and fosters a positive outlook, even during challenging times. It also enhances group performance by promoting cooperation, mitigating conflict, and sustaining collective energy. Strategies for improving team spirit include building trust and psychological safety, recognizing contributions, fostering a shared purpose, encouraging open communication, establishing meaningful traditions, and providing opportunities for social connection and shared decision-making. When nurtured with intention, team spirit becomes a powerful force for unity, engagement, and group success.

Chapter 19
We Resolve Conflict in Positive Ways

RESOLVING CONFLICT IN positive ways involves addressing disagreements constructively. This means aiming to strengthen relationships, foster understanding, and promote mutual growth. Instead of avoiding or escalating disputes, favorable conflict resolution emphasizes collaboration, empathy, and open communication to find solutions that satisfy all parties involved. This approach to conflict resolution takes various forms, such as:

- Engaging in honest dialogue where each party feels heard and respected. This involves active listening, expressing thoughts clearly, and avoiding blame or personal attacks.
- Managing emotions to prevent escalation. Taking a moment to calm down before responding can lead to more thoughtful discussions.
- Striving to see the situation from the other person's perspective. This helps find common ground and resolve misunderstandings.

- Collaborating to identify underlying issues and develop mutually beneficial solutions.
- Involving a neutral third party to facilitate the resolution of persistent conflicts by providing an unbiased perspective and guiding the conversation constructively.

Resolving conflict in a healthy and constructive manner enables individuals or groups to address disagreements without damaging relationships or undermining shared goals. Effective conflict resolution is characterized by respect, emotional maturity, and a commitment to maintaining strong, positive relationships, even in the face of disagreements. It strengthens bonds and builds resilience for future challenges. Here's what that looks like in households, workplaces, and communities:

Households
- Family members discuss disagreements calmly and respectfully, avoiding yelling, withdrawal, or holding grudges.
- Everyone's feelings and perspectives are heard and taken seriously, especially children's voices, in age-appropriate ways.
- Family members are willing to adjust, negotiate, and find middle ground.
- After a conflict, there's a process of reconnecting—through apologies, gestures of goodwill, or shared activities—to restore closeness.

Workplaces
- Team members express their concerns directly yet tactfully, focusing on behaviors or issues rather than making personal attacks.

- Conflict is viewed as an opportunity to enhance systems or clarify misunderstandings, rather than assigning blame.
- The organization has established structures, such as HR mediation and team protocols, to resolve disputes fairly.
- Even in the face of disagreements, coworkers maintain professionalism, trust, and collaboration.

Communities

- Residents discuss contentious issues (e.g., zoning, safety, or cultural differences) in forums, town halls, or informal settings where diverse voices are heard and considered.
- There are agreed-upon norms for engaging respectfully, even during disagreements.
- Trusted leaders or trained mediators assist in resolving conflicts between groups or individuals while respecting all parties involved.
- After a conflict, community members strive to restore a sense of unity through collaborative projects, healing events, or joint planning efforts.

Failing to resolve conflicts positively within a subculture can result in fragmentation, hostility, and decline.

- Unresolved tensions can escalate, resulting in open hostility or even physical confrontations.
- When conflicts are poorly managed, subcultures can emerge that resist change, cultivate negativity, and weaken organizational goals.
- Unresolved conflict undermines trust among members and results in the breakdown of communication.
- Subcultures may establish their identity in contrast to others, fostering a mentality of "us versus them.".

- The media's portrayal of subcultural conflicts can amplify stereotypes.
- Dominant groups may suppress dissenting voices, resulting in a culture that is homogenized and stifles creativity and innovation.

> **Tip: Subcultures Vary in Their Approach to Conflict**
>
> Subcultures differ in their tolerance and approach to conflict. These differences influence whether conflict is perceived as an opportunity for growth or a threat to group cohesion, and they shape the strategies used for conflict resolution. In some subcultures, a good argument is a form of expressing love and connection. In other subcultures, even minor conflicts can feel overwhelming. Individualistic subcultures (e.g., many Western societies) often value assertiveness, direct communication, and open confrontation. Collectivistic subcultures (e.g., many Asian or Latin American communities) prioritize group harmony and may avoid direct conflict. Subcultures that value hierarchy may discourage open disagreement with authority. Understanding these subcultural differences is crucial in multicultural settings. For instance, in organizational environments, it is important to recognize that team members may have different conflict resolution preferences.

Implications for a Positive Outlook

Conflict resolution turns potential obstacles into pathways for personal and collective growth. By viewing conflicts as opportunities to learn and connect, individuals develop a more positive and resilient mindset, which in turn improves both personal well-being and interpersonal relationships. Here's how a positive approach to conflict resolution contributes:

- **Promotes a Growth Mindset:** Approaching conflicts constructively encourages individuals to see challenges as opportunities for learning and development. This shift in mindset reduces fear and defensiveness, allowing people to embrace change and pursue personal growth.
- **Encourages Innovation and Problem-Solving:** Constructive conflict can stimulate critical thinking and creativity. By challenging existing ideas and encouraging diverse viewpoints, conflict resolution can lead to innovative solutions and improved decision-making.
- **Enhances Communication and Empathy:** Effective conflict resolution requires active listening and empathetic engagement. By understanding differing perspectives, individuals can foster deeper connections and trust, leading to more meaningful and supportive relationships.
- **Reduces Stress and Builds Resilience:** Proactively addressing conflicts prevents unresolved tensions from accumulating, which can otherwise lead to stress and anxiety. Developing conflict resolution skills provides individuals with tools to navigate future disagreements more calmly and confidently.
- **Strengthens Relationships:** Successfully resolving conflicts can deepen mutual respect and understanding between parties, thereby enhancing the value of collaboration and shared goals and contributing to more harmonious and lasting relationships.

Chapter 19

Myths and Misunderstandings about Having High Team Spirit

A positive approach to conflict resolution is often misunderstood, leading to myths that can hinder effective communication and hamper growth. By debunking these misconceptions, we can leverage conflict as a catalyst for personal and group development.

Myth/ Misunderstanding	Reality
Conflict is inherently harmful and should be avoided.	While conflict can be uncomfortable, it isn't inherently bad. When managed constructively, conflict can foster innovation, enhance understanding, and strengthen relationships. Avoiding conflict often lets underlying issues fester, which can lead to greater problems down the line.
All conflicts can and should be resolved.	Not all conflicts are resolvable, especially when they arise from deeply held values or beliefs. In these instances, the goal shifts from resolution to respectful coexistence, acknowledging differences without hostility.
Effective conflict resolution always results in a win-win outcome.	While collaborative solutions are ideal, they aren't always practical. Sometimes, compromise or respectfully agreeing to disagree is the most feasible outcome. The key lies in open communication and mutual respect, even when complete agreement isn't achievable.
Conflict indicates poor leadership or dysfunctional relationships.	Conflict is a natural part of any dynamic relationship or subculture. Effective leaders recognize this and promote environments where conflicts are resolved constructively, leading to growth and improvement.
Avoiding conflict maintains harmony.	Suppressing conflict does not eliminate it; it often intensifies tensions. Addressing issues openly prevents resentment and fosters genuine harmony.

Strategies for Fostering Positive Approaches to Conflict

The goal is to create environments that encourage open communication, mutual respect, and collaborative problem-solving. By proactively addressing conflicts, we can improve team dynamics, boost morale, and enhance overall productivity. There are many effective strategies for supporting conflict resolution within a subculture, including:

- **Learn Conflict Resolution Skills:** Focusing on active listening, empathy, and effective communication empowers individuals to navigate disagreements constructively and resolve conflicts effectively.
- **Develop Policies and Procedures Regarding Conflict:** Communicating clear policies for addressing conflict ensures consistency and fairness. These guidelines should outline the steps for reporting issues, mediation processes, and potential resolutions. A structured approach to conflict management demystifies the process and encourages individuals to address issues promptly.
- **Encourage Open Communication:** Encouraging transparency and open dialogue helps identify and resolve conflicts early. Regular meetings, feedback sessions, and open-door policies foster a safe environment where people can voice their concerns and collaborate on finding solutions.
- **Offer Mediation and Third-Party Facilitation:** In situations where internal resolution proves to be challenging, involving neutral third-party mediators can be beneficial. External facilitators provide objectivity and can guide parties toward mutually agreeable solutions, especially in complex or sensitive disputes.
- **Encourage Collaborative Problem-Solving:** Such approaches highlight common goals and foster mutual respect. Methods

such as joint brainstorming and consensus-building can lead to innovative solutions and foster team cohesion.
- **Address Serial Offenders:** Some individuals struggle to adopt a positive approach to conflict resolution, thereby exacerbating conflicts by being uncooperative, aggressive, or unwilling to acknowledge and address issues. In such cases, it may be necessary to limit the impact of these individuals or groups by modifying their roles and responsibilities.
- **Monitor and Evaluate Conflict Resolution Efforts:** Regularly assessing the level of perceived conflict and whether conflicts are being resolved effectively can identify necessary adjustments. Collecting feedback, tracking resolution outcomes, and analyzing patterns can inform policy updates.

Summing Up

Successful conflict resolution is the process of addressing disagreements constructively, focusing on understanding diverse perspectives, strengthening relationships, and finding mutually beneficial solutions. Instead of avoiding or escalating conflict, this approach emphasizes empathy, respectful communication, emotional regulation, and collaborative problem-solving. It is vital because unresolved or mismanaged conflict can lead to mistrust, decreased morale, and dysfunction, while constructive resolution fosters psychological safety, trust, and innovation. To foster subcultures that promote positive conflict resolution, groups can encourage open dialogue, provide training, establish clear conflict resolution policies, model respectful behavior, and promote shared responsibility for maintaining healthy interpersonal dynamics. These efforts help normalize conflict as a pathway to growth rather than a threat to cohesion.

Chapter 20

We Celebrate Achievements

IN A SUBCULTURE that celebrates achievements, people recognize, honor, and take pride in both individual and collective accomplishments. These celebrations can take many forms, including verbal praise, awards, rituals, events, public acknowledgments, and informal expressions of appreciation. Here's what it can look like in practice:

- A workplace hosting a team lunch to mark the successful completion of a project.
- A neighborhood newsletter highlighting the contributions of community volunteers.
- A family expressing joy and pride when a member graduates or gets a promotion.
- A classroom displaying student work or offering certificates for progress.

People celebrate in various ways, influenced by cultural traditions, personal preferences, and the nature of the occasion.

Chapter 20

Celebration serves to strengthen relationships, reinforce values, and promote joy and gratitude. Whether shared or solitary, elaborate or simple, celebrations create emotional connections and lasting memories. Here are some familiar and meaningful ways that people celebrate:

- Celebrating birthdays, graduations, weddings, and holidays with food, music, and dancing.
- Sharing meals at home or in restaurants to mark achievements or milestones.
- Organizing formal events like award ceremonies, baptisms, or retirement send-offs.
- Offering presents, cards, or flowers to express appreciation or joy.
- Acknowledging someone's accomplishments or contributions with words of praise.
- Lighting candles or fireworks to commemorate significant events.
- Including cultural or religious rites at weddings, coming-of-age rituals, or holiday customs.
- Giving awards and honors such as plaques, certificates, or public shout-outs in meetings or media.
- Sharing accomplishments or joyful moments online to involve others.
- Organizing community events such as parades, festivals, or public displays to celebrate group or civic pride.
- Volunteering or donating by giving time or resources in honor of someone or something.
- Helping others celebrate by joining in another's joy by participating or offering support.

- Dancing, singing, or playing music to express joy through movement and sound.
- Using art or storytelling to capture the meaning of the celebration.
- Celebrating by taking a break or vacation to enjoy rest or adventure.
- Treating oneself to a special meal, spa day, or personal gift to celebrate an occasion or accomplishment.

When a subculture fails to celebrate achievements, it implies that the group tends to ignore, downplay, or overlook both individual and collective successes. Praise may be infrequent, muted, or inconsistent.

Implications for a Positive Outlook

Celebrating achievements plays an important role in fostering a positive outlook by:

Promoting Positivity: Acknowledging achievements, regardless of their size, demonstrates that goals are attainable and progress is being made. This reinforces the belief that future success is achievable, a crucial factor in maintaining a positive outlook.

Increasing Confidence: Celebration affirms people's capabilities, sending the messages such as, "We're capable, we're moving forward, and we're making a difference." This collective confidence helps individuals and groups approach challenges with resilience and optimism.

Countering Negativity: By intentionally focusing on what's going well, celebrations can counterbalance negative stressors and setbacks. This shift in focus helps reframe challenges as part of a broader pattern of growth and success.

Fostering Gratitude: Celebrations often highlight teamwork, support, and effort, cultivating appreciation for others and the journey, not just the outcomes. Gratitude is closely linked to a more positive, hopeful mindset.

Creating Shared Joy: Group celebrations foster emotionally uplifting experiences that enhance social bonds and contribute to a collective sense of well-being, belonging, and pride—all of which support a sustained positive outlook.

Myths and Misunderstandings about Celebrating Accomplishments

Celebrating accomplishments is often misunderstood, creating myths that can diminish their positive impact. Here are some of the more problematic myths and misconceptions:

Myth/ Misunderstanding	Reality
Celebration breeds complacency.	Celebrating achievements reinforces motivation and highlights the behaviors and values worth repeating.
Only big wins deserve recognition.	Celebrating small wins helps maintain momentum, morale, and a growth mindset over time.
People should be intrinsically motivated.	While it's important that people be internally motivated, external affirmation enhances it by helping people feel seen and valued.
It's not professional to celebrate.	Thoughtful celebration—such as a thank-you, public acknowledgment, or reflection—builds professionalism by strengthening engagement and team spirit.

Myth/ Misunderstanding	Reality
Everyone already knows they're appreciated.	People often need explicit affirmation. Otherwise, their efforts can feel unnoticed or taken for granted.
When it comes to celebrating, one size fits all.	People have preferences for how they would like to be celebrated, including the level of publicness they prefer, who they want to celebrate with, and the form of celebration or acknowledgement they like.

Strategies for Fostering Subcultures that Celebrate Achievements

There are multiple strategies for increasing the quality and frequency of celebrations while making them meaningful:

- Highlight team accomplishments and collaborative wins to build cohesion.
- Give the celebration extra meaning by tying it to your group's purpose, values, or goals.
- Reinforce shared identity and progress toward common goals.
- Encourage noticing and sharing everyday successes, not just major milestones.
- Create rituals for recognizing effort, growth, or progress (e.g., "shout-outs" and weekly wins).
- Use verbal forms of recognition, such as saying "Great job on..." or offering public praise in meetings.
- Communicate your recognition through notes, emails, or on bulletin boards.
- Make recognition visible by displaying your appreciation in photos or charts.

- Share accomplishments in newsletters or on social media (if appropriate).
- Invite everyone, not just leaders, to participate in recognizing others.
- Create a rotating "recognition role" to highlight peers' contributions.
- Start meetings with a recognition of contribution or success.
- Mark milestones such as anniversaries, personal successes, and completing projects.
- Schedule group events tied to accomplishments (e.g., a team lunch or virtual coffee break).
- Offer guidance on giving authentic praise and celebrating inclusively.
- Encourage leaders to model appreciation in a visible and consistent manner.
- Avoid superficial or generic praise.
- Tie recognition to specific actions, values, or results.

Summing Up

Celebrating achievements involves recognizing and appreciating both individual and group successes, whether large or small, in a manner that reinforces shared values and fosters a sense of pride and accomplishment. This practice is essential in subcultures as it enhances motivation, encourages a sense of progress, and strengthens social connections. Recognizing accomplishments is crucial in cultivating a positive outlook, as it fosters optimism, builds confidence, and nurtures gratitude. It shifts focus from challenges to progress, enabling individuals and groups to view themselves as capable and resilient.

For maximum effectiveness, celebrations should be intentional, inclusive, and integrated into the group's routine. This encompasses recognizing small wins, encouraging peer-to-peer appreciation, utilizing various recognition methods, and aligning celebrations with core goals and values. Both leaders and members should demonstrate authentic acknowledgment, making it a natural and valued aspect of the culture.

Chapter 21

We Have a Can-Do Attitude

SUBCULTURES CAN ADOPT a can-do attitude when their shared beliefs, behaviors, and norms promote confidence, persistence, and problem-solving. This type of subculture fosters a mindset characterized by optimism, determination, and confidence in one's ability to overcome challenges and achieve goals. With a can-do attitude, members:

- Focus on solutions rather than obstacles.
- Take initiative and embrace responsibility.
- Persist in the face of setbacks.
- Display confidence in themselves and their team.
- Maintain a positive outlook, even under pressure.

This attitude often results in greater resilience, improved problem-solving, and enhanced group morale. It is particularly valuable in group environments, where it nurtures momentum and a culture of possibility.

Chapter 21

Subcultures with a can-do attitude in households, workplaces, and communities tend to exhibit resilience, initiative, collaboration, and a forward-looking spirit. Here are examples of what this might look like in each setting:

Households
- **Problem-solving together:** Family members address issues such as a broken appliance or tight finances by brainstorming solutions instead of assigning blame or giving up.
- **Encouraging independence and growth:** Parents foster confidence in children by saying things like, "Let's figure it out together," rather than shielding them from all challenges.
- **Resilience in adversity:** After setbacks such as a job loss or illness, family members move into action mode, supporting one another both emotionally and practically.

Workplaces
- **Culture of Innovation and improvement:** Employees do not wait for permission to suggest improvements or take the initiative on new projects—they act and iterate.
- **Strong morale in times of change:** During restructuring or under high-pressure deadlines, people sustain their energy and discover ways to adapt, driven by confidence that "we can handle this."
- **Supportive peer behavior:** Colleagues uplift and assist one another, reinforcing effort and perseverance instead of defeatism.

Communities

- **Rapid mobilization of volunteers:** People work together to respond quickly and effectively to crises such as natural disasters or economic hardship.
- **Local problem-solving:** Residents address shared concerns (e.g., traffic safety, access to fresh food) with initiative, by petitioning officials, organizing cooperatives, or launching local campaigns.
- **Inclusive participation:** People believe their voice matters and they act on it, whether by attending town meetings or contributing to local projects.

When subcultures lack a can-do attitude, they often experience stagnation, low morale, and a reduced ability to cope with challenges. People tend to ignore problems or postpone addressing them, hoping they will resolve themselves instead of facing them head-on. This fear of failure or the belief that trying is futile leads to diminished self-confidence. Setbacks trigger finger-pointing or a sense that "nothing can be done," which can undermine trust and collaboration. People may hide mistakes and avoid accountability.

Implications for a Positive Outlook

A can-do attitude plays a central role in fostering a positive outlook by shaping how individuals and groups interpret challenges and opportunities. This attitude nurtures a sense of agency, fuels optimism, and helps individuals and groups remain hopeful, active, and engaged, even in the face of adversity. Here's how it contributes:

- **Builds Confidence in the Future:** Problems can be solved, and goals can be achieved, which fosters hope and motivation.

This forward-looking confidence enables people to see possibilities rather than just obstacles.
- **Encourages Constructive Action:** A can-do mindset transforms setbacks into action, rather than defeat. Even small actions strengthen a sense of control and optimism.
- **Promotes Resilience:** When people believe they can adapt and overcome, they bounce back more quickly from adversity. This resilience strengthens both individual and collective morale.
- **Fosters Group Energy and Morale:** In teams or communities, a can-do spirit fosters momentum and encourages collective optimism. People are more likely to support each other and contribute when they believe success is achievable.
- **Counters Cynicism and Helplessness:** A can-do attitude disrupts negative thinking patterns by emphasizing solutions and growth. This helps prevent a spiral into pessimism, blame, or withdrawal.

Myths and Misunderstandings about Having a Can-Do Attitude

There are several myths and misunderstandings about a can-do attitude that can undermine its appeal and ability to support a positive outlook. Here are some of the more problematic myths and misconceptions.

Myth/Misunderstanding	Reality
A can-do attitude means ignoring problems or pretending everything is fine.	A genuine can-do mindset recognizes difficulties but emphasizes finding constructive responses. It's not about denial or false positivity.

Myth/Misunderstanding	Reality
People either have a can-do attitude or they don't.	This mindset can be cultivated and developed through encouragement, supportive environments, and consistent practice.
A can-do attitude is about working harder, no matter what.	It's not about constant hustle or burnout. It's about working smarter, remaining flexible, and adapting to challenges with creativity and determination.
A can-do attitude guarantees success.	While it increases the chances of success, it doesn't eliminate external barriers or guarantee results. It's a mindset that improves the approach, not a magic solution.
Can-do attitudes are only helpful in work or goal-setting situations.	They are important in emotional resilience, relationships, family life, and community engagement, where persistence, hope, and problem-solving are significant factors.
People with a can-do attitude never feel discouraged.	They face doubts and setbacks, yet they choose to persist and reframe challenges instead of giving up.

Strategies for Creating Subcultures with a Can-Do Attitude

There are several strategies to increase the frequency of can-do attitudes within a subculture. Here are some of the most effective ones:

- Leaders and role models can showcase perseverance, solution-oriented thinking, and constructive approaches to challenges.
- Normalize talking through setbacks and brainstorming next steps.

- Recognize not only successes but also persistence, creative problem-solving, and teamwork.
- Publicly affirm small wins to build momentum and morale.
- Encourage a mindset shift from "this is a problem" to "this is a challenge we can meet."
- Use uplifting language such as "What can we try?" or "How might we move forward?"
- Assist groups in defining what success looks like and how to achieve it in a step-by-step manner.
- Break large tasks into manageable parts to prevent overwhelm and build confidence.
- Tell true, relatable stories of past successes, resilience, and growth within the group.
- Design systems that reward initiative and allow room for experimentation.

Summing Up

A "can-do" attitude is a mindset characterized by optimism, persistence, and the belief that challenges can be overcome through effort, creativity, and collaboration. It plays a crucial role in fostering a positive outlook by promoting confidence in the future, encouraging action in the face of obstacles, and reinforcing the belief that progress is possible. When shared within a subculture—such as a household, workplace, or community—it helps individuals and groups remain hopeful, resilient, and engaged. A can-do attitude can be nurtured by modeling constructive responses to setbacks, celebrating effort and progress, involving people in problem-solving, setting clear and achievable goals, and creating a supportive environment where individuals feel empowered and encouraged to contribute.

Chapter 22

We Are Proud

TAKING PRIDE IN our group involves experiencing a sense of satisfaction, loyalty, and a personal connection to the group's identity, values, and achievements. It reflects a belief that the group is valuable, capable, and represents something meaningful. Group pride often manifests in behaviors such as celebrating milestones, displaying symbols (e.g., logos, slogans), defending the group's reputation, or going the extra mile to contribute. It strengthens commitment, fosters unity, and boosts morale.

Here are examples of how pride in the group manifests itself in households, workplaces, and neighborhoods:

Households

- Displaying family photos, awards, or heirlooms honors shared history.
- Telling stories about family resilience or success (e.g., "Your grandmother built this house with her own hands.").
- Hosting or attending family reunions and traditions that celebrate family togetherness.

- Working together to keep the house clean and well-maintained reflects our shared responsibility and pride in our home.

Workplaces
- Wearing company-branded clothing or using branded items.
- Celebrating team successes, including project completions, awards, and milestone achievements.
- Referring others to apply to or do business with the organization, showing confidence in its value.
- Taking initiative to improve systems or solve problems because people care about the group's performance and reputation.

Communities
- Participating in community clean-ups, events, or improvement projects like garden builds or mural paintings.
- Welcoming new neighbors warmly and involving them in local traditions or block parties.
- Displaying local symbols such as flags, banners, or sports team memorabilia.
- Defending the neighborhood's reputation in conversation or online, and speaking positively about its culture and people.

Lacking pride in the group means feeling disconnected, indifferent, or even ashamed of being associated with it. This reflects a lack of emotional investment, low identification with the group's values or reputation, and minimal motivation to contribute to its well-being or success. Here's what it can look like in different settings:

Households

- Avoiding family time or traditions, showing little interest in shared activities or celebrations.
- Speaking negatively about family members or minimizing their accomplishments.
- Neglecting the living space, showing no concern for its appearance or upkeep.
- Feeling embarrassed by or hiding one's family background in social settings.

Workplaces

- Doing the bare minimum, with no sense of responsibility for group success.
- Speaking poorly of the organization to others or actively discouraging others from joining.
- Avoiding participation in team meetings, events, or improvements.
- Withholding effort or innovation, especially if success doesn't feel personally meaningful.

Communities

- Disengaging from neighbors or local events, treating the neighborhood as temporary or unworthy of investment.
- Letting property fall into disrepair, showing a lack of concern for community standards.
- Complaining about the neighborhood, even when improvements are possible.
- Not making an effort to connect with or support fellow residents (e.g., ignoring issues that affect everyone).

Chapter 22

Implications for a Positive Outlook

Pride serves as a cultural amplifier of positivity, deepening connections, igniting enthusiasm, and sustaining hope. Without it, even talented or well-intentioned groups can miss growth opportunities, become discouraged, or become disjointed. Having pride in a subculture has significant implications for fostering a positive outlook among its members. It can:

- **Enhance Optimism and Hope:** When people feel proud of their group, they are more likely to believe in its potential to succeed, overcome challenges, and improve. This fuels a forward-looking mindset and reinforces the belief that "we can make things better."
- **Boost Motivation and Engagement:** Pride fosters a deeper emotional investment. People care more, try harder, and are more willing to contribute because they see their efforts as part of something meaningful and worthwhile.
- **Build\ Resilience During Difficult Times:** A proud group is more likely to rally together in the face of adversity. Members are more supportive of each other and maintain confidence that the group will recover or adapt.
- **Strengthen Group Identity and Belonging:** Pride reinforces a shared identity. Feeling like "this is my team, my family, my community" increases commitment and cohesion, which are key for a positive outlook.
- **Encourage a Culture of Recognition:** When pride exists, achievements-big or small—tend to be acknowledged and celebrated. This reinforces positivity and helps individuals feel valued and appreciated.
- **Reduce Cynicism and Complaining:** Pride shifts focus from what's wrong to what's working. It creates a sense of

gratitude and satisfaction that helps balance out negativity or apathy.

Myths and Misunderstandings About Having Group Pride

Several myths and misunderstandings can limit the positive benefits of pride within groups. By addressing the following myths, groups can cultivate a healthy, inclusive, and motivating sense of pride that fosters a positive outlook.

Myth/ Misunderstanding	Reality
Pride leads to arrogance or superiority.	Healthy pride is about appreciation and respect, not superiority. It builds confidence and connection without putting others down.
Pride should only come after significant achievements.	Pride can and should be built from everyday efforts, shared values, progress, and positive relationships, not just big wins.
Expressing pride is boastful or unprofessional.	When done with humility, expressing pride fosters team morale, identity, and motivation, not ego.
Pride hides problems or discourages growth.	Real pride often includes constructive reflection and a desire to improve. It's possible to be proud and still strive to grow.
Pride must be unanimous to be valid.	Pride can start with a few people who care deeply. Their energy can inspire others and gradually transform the culture.
Pride is an individual emotion, not a collective one.	Pride in a group is a shared emotional connection that boosts trust, unity, and commitment among its members.

Chapter 22

Strategies for Fostering Pride Within a Subculture

Strategies for fostering pride enhance shared identity, acknowledge contributions, and reinforce the group's value. Here are some effective strategies:

- Recognize both individual and group successes—big and small.
- Hold ceremonies, meetings, or informal gatherings to mark achievements.
- Share stories of perseverance and positive impact.
- Reaffirm what the group stands for and why it matters.
- Use symbols (e.g., logos, mottos, traditions) to reinforce identity.
- Tell origin stories or talk about milestones that reflect core values.
- Involve members in setting goals and solving problems.
- Give everyone meaningful roles and responsibilities.
- Encourage suggestions and act on group input.
- Display shared accomplishments (e.g., photos, art, awards).
- Encourage group symbols, such as team shirts, signs, and hashtags, to promote unity and camaraderie.
- Maintain the physical environment with care and intention.
- Share uplifting anecdotes, challenges that have been overcome, and moments of unity.
- Use newsletters, meetings, or social media to tell these stories.
- Highlight group heroes—past and present.
- Create opportunities for bonding through celebrations, outings, and shared projects.
- Support acts of kindness and mutual aid.

- Leaders should express genuine pride in the group.
- Acknowledge efforts publicly and often.
- Speak positively about the group both within and outside of the organization.
- Reflect on how far the group has come.
- Use visual tools (e.g., timelines, scrapbooks, highlight reels).
- Invite reflection on what makes the group special or unique.

When pride is nurtured through practices such as these, it becomes self-reinforcing. This boosts morale, strengthens identity, and fosters a resilient and positive outlook.

Summing Up

Group pride is a shared sense of respect, satisfaction, and emotional connection to one's household, workplace, or community. It reflects the belief that the group is valuable, capable, and worth being part of. This pride strengthens a positive culture by boosting morale, deepening commitment, and reinforcing a shared identity. It encourages members to contribute, support one another, and celebrate collective achievements, which in turn fosters optimism, a sense of belonging, and resilience. Group pride can be achieved through recognizing accomplishments, affirming shared values, involving members in meaningful ways, encouraging positive storytelling, and creating visible symbols of group identity. When nurtured consistently, pride becomes a cultural force that uplifts both individual and group well-being.

Now Is the Time to Strengthen Our Social Climate

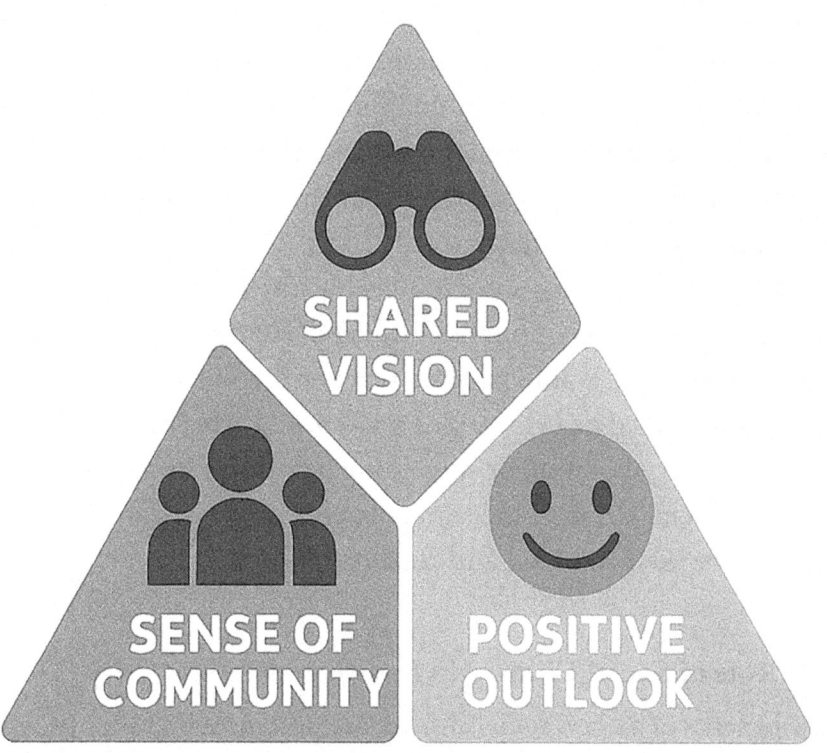

Right now, we face a critical crossroads on many fronts. Will we choose authoritarian leadership styles in the workplace, at home, and in government? Will we tackle the loneliness epidemic and the health care crisis? Will we adopt healthier lifestyles? How will we manage rapid technological changes? We urgently need supportive social climates to tackle these and other unforeseen challenges.

The Role of Social Climate in Bringing About Lasting and Positive Cultural Change

At the Human Resources Institute, our work focuses on the role of social climate in enabling groups and organizations to achieve desired and lasting cultural change. This goal has led us to discover that a sense of community, a shared vision, and a positive outlook are critical enabling factors in our work. We recognize the need to consider the social climate in our proposals. At the very least, we understand that the recommended changes must improve, not undermine, the social climate.

When these elements are noticeably absent, achieving change becomes difficult, if not impossible. People may resist change, even when the changes would benefit everyone involved. Incentives can be misinterpreted as bribes. Good intentions may be perceived as manipulation, coercion, or something nefarious. In contrast, with a strong social climate, the same proposals and actions are more likely to be well-received and readily adopted.

The Role of Social Climate in Health and Productivity

The benefits of a good social climate are unique in that they provide both improved health and productivity. This dual benefit makes it particularly attractive. The research supporting the health benefits of positive social connections is among the most conclusive in the social sciences. Dr. Dean Ornish, president and founder of the nonprofit Preventive Medicine Research Institute, summarized his review of more than 100 studies: "I am not aware of any other factor in medicine—not diet, not smoking, not exercise, not stress, not genetics, not drugs, not surgery—that has a greater impact on our quality of life, incidence of illness, and premature death from all causes."

Don Cohen and Laurence Prusak offer a comprehensive review of this supportive literature in their groundbreaking book, *In Good Company: How Social Capital Makes Organizations Work*. These authors identify four core primary benefits of social capital. Although their review focused on business outcomes, it is clear that the productivity benefits also translate to positive outcomes for households and other groups. According to Cohen and Prusak, favorable relationships enhance business outcomes by:

- **Increasing knowledge sharing.** People are more likely to share their best ideas when they get along and are enthusiastic about their goals. They are also more likely to seek opportunities to implement these ideas. Social networks increase the likelihood that various perspectives are considered in important decisions.
- **Increasing the coherence of action.** Successful organizations follow through on their plans. Good ideas are executed in a way that fully benefits the group or organization. On an individual level, a supportive social climate increases the likelihood that people will achieve their professional development goals and maintain healthier lifestyles.

- **Reducing transaction costs.** Mutual trust eliminates the need for lawyers. Trust also minimizes the likelihood of internal disagreements disrupting performance. In business, customers and suppliers can engage with each other through a handshake. They will also remain attentive to improving work processes and future outcomes.
- **Reducing employment costs.** Employers discover that having a reputation as a great place to work makes it easier to attract talent. Employees become effective recruiters and are likely to stay even when work becomes challenging. A supportive social climate reduces the likelihood of accidents, injuries, and illnesses.

The Role of Social Climate in Successful Health Promotion and Wellness Programs

Over the past forty years, I have observed the evolution of wellness programs in workplaces and communities. Unfortunately, many of these programs failed to consider the social climate adequately. For example:

- Lifestyle assessments have focused on health risks and their impact on life expectancy. These fear-based, deficit-oriented approaches undermine the positive perspective.
- Many wellness programs have focused on controlling health care costs, rather than highlighting the positive effects of improved performance and quality of life. The implication is that employees' unhealthy behaviors are responsible for high health care costs. This blame-shifting has had little impact on encouraging employees to adopt healthier habits. The negative focus undermines the social climate.

- In the 1970s, corporate wellness programs provided support groups and fitness facilities. They highlighted the importance of peer support and methods for achieving wellness through fun runs and other activities with coworkers. The support groups aimed to tackle a range of issues, including quitting smoking, losing weight, and managing stress. These early programs have since transformed into initiatives that prioritize individual change. Computers have enabled the personalization of health information for all. Wellness coaches help facilitate personal change. This shift towards individual change has unintentionally diminished the social benefits of the original wellness programs.

Wellness programs need to be reimagined to improve the social climate. The focus should shift towards fostering and nurturing social connections. The fear of illness and economic loss must be deemphasized and replaced with goals centered on mutual support and overall well-being. Integrating households, groups, and community engagement should also be a key component of program design.

The Role of Social Climate in Addressing Our Current Loneliness Epidemic

The loneliness epidemic refers to a widespread and growing public health issue where a significant portion of the population experiences chronic loneliness and social isolation. It has gained global attention due to its adverse effects on mental, emotional, and physical health, as well as its impact on societal well-being. Nearly one in two adults in the U.S. report feeling lonely. Chronic loneliness is associated with:

- Increased risk of depression, anxiety, and suicide
- Weakened immune system
- Cardiovascular disease
- Cognitive decline and dementia
- Shortened life expectancy
- Higher rates of emergency room visits and hospitalization
- Workplace absenteeism and loss of productivity
- Higher healthcare costs
- Reduced civic engagement

Measuring loneliness and its consequences among individuals is standard practice; however, solutions should not rely solely on individual change. An effective approach to addressing this epidemic involves cultural change at the group, organizational, and community levels.

Increased social interactions will benefit us little if they are toxic. A stronger social climate can enhance both the quantity and quality of our social connections. When there is a shared vision, people have reasons to come together. When there is a positive outlook, people can enjoy and celebrate their relationships. When there is a sense of community, people trust one another and feel comfortable in groups.

The Role of Social Climate in Technological Innovation

New technologies can both bring us together and weaken social connections. We must harness their advantages while tackling their drawbacks. Below is a table outlining the opportunities and challenges that current innovations present.

Technology & Social Connection: Help vs. Harm

Area	How Technology Helps	How Technology Hurts
Communication	Instant messaging and video calls keep people connected	Can lead to shallow, surface-level interaction
Relationships	Reconnects old friends, maintains long-distance bonds	Promotes social comparison and FOMO (fear of missing out)
Community Building	Online groups and movements build belonging around shared values	Reduces real-world community involvement and civic engagement
Emotional Support	Online peer support, therapy apps, and support groups make emotional support accessible	Can replace in-person care, risking depersonalization
Collaboration & Teamwork	Remote work tools enable collaboration	Can erode interpersonal trust and spontaneity in teams
Accessibility	Online platforms can connect people with disabilities or those who are isolated	May leave behind those without access or digital literacy
Presence & Mindfulness	Mindfulness apps and journaling tools can help people cultivate presence	Notifications and constant connectivity fragment attention
Diversity & Empathy	Exposure to different cultures and viewpoints promotes empathy	Algorithms may polarize political positions and create echo chambers

In supportive cultures, technology serves as a tool to strengthen connections, deepen shared meaning, and mobilize collective energy. Whether it's a household FaceTime call, a workplace Slack channel, or an online grassroots campaign, the thoughtful use of technology helps people feel that they belong, are valued, and are part of a real community. These digital connections can form essential building blocks of a thriving social climate.

The Role of Social Climate in Resisting Authoritarian Culture

In an authoritarian culture, power, control, and decision-making are concentrated in the hands of a few individuals or a central authority, with expectations of strict obedience and conformity from members, often enforced through fear, surveillance, or punishment, and with little tolerance for dissent or participation in the decision-making process. Authoritarianism appears in different forms:

- **Workplaces:**
  - Micromanagement and "command and control" practices.
  - Leaders discourage feedback, enforce rules strictly, and discourage questioning.
- **Households:**
  - Parents dictate all decisions; children have no input or voice.
  - Punishments for minor infractions, with strict obedience expected.
- **Communities or societies:**
  - The government suppresses press freedom and punishes critics.
  - Surveillance is used to enforce ideological conformity.

A supportive social climate reduces the likelihood that subcultures will develop into authoritarian groups. Here are some ways a sense of community, shared vision, and a positive outlook can counter authoritarianism:

- **Strengthens trust and psychological safety:** Authoritarian cultures thrive on fear and distrust to maintain control. A supportive social climate fosters trust, openness, and psychological safety, reducing the fear-based conditions that make authoritarian control appealing or possible.
- **Encourages participation and shared decision-making:** Authoritarian cultures centralize power and discourage input. A supportive social climate normalizes involvement, dialogue, and shared ownership, making it culturally unacceptable for decisions to be imposed unilaterally.
- **Builds social connections and solidarity:** Authoritarian leaders exploit social isolation, offering a sense of belonging in exchange for obedience and conformity. Supportive climates foster genuine social connections and collective identity, fulfilling belonging needs in healthy ways and reducing susceptibility to authoritarian promises.
- **Promotes critical thinking and dissent:** Authoritarian cultures often suppress dissent and critical questioning. In a supportive climate, disagreement and diverse viewpoints are welcomed, allowing issues to surface before they can be exploited by those seeking control.
- **Reduces fear during uncertainty:** Crises and uncertainty often lead people to accept authoritarian control as a perceived means of safety. A supportive social climate provides mutual aid, clear communication, and collective problem-solving, reducing fear and the desire for a "strongman" solution.

You Can Value Social Climate

Social climate is often overlooked in highly individualistic cultures, particularly those that prioritize personal achievement, autonomy, and self-expression over collective well-being and mutual responsibility. Social climate tends to fluctuate in waves over time within cultures. Economic conditions, political factors, technological changes, cultural narratives, and social movements influence these shifts.

Hopefully, this book has helped you to identify one or more opportunities to enhance the social climate in your group(s). There is no perfect formula, and the social climate manifests in various ways across households, workplaces, and communities. Utilizing the *Social Climate Indicator* from Chapter 2 on an annual or biannual basis could provide feedback on past efforts to enhance the social climate and offer insights into areas that may require further attention. Ideally, you will ask the members of your group or organization about their perceptions of the social climate and the changes needed. Achieving almost any change will depend on the support and engagement of group members. Involve them in setting goals and implementing strategies, as people typically do not respond well to changes made without their involvement.

It is unlikely that implementing a single recommendation will lead to the desired and sustained change. Most cultural changes happen when a cluster of influences shifts the culture toward a new attitude or behavior. Consider this when addressing the twenty attitudes and behaviors explored in this section. Each chapter presents multiple strategic recommendations. Implement at least four of these recommendations to shift the culture effectively.

Good Social Skills Are No Substitute for Strengthening the Social Climate in Subcultures

This book emphasizes strategies that can improve the social climate in households, workplaces, and communities. A complementary approach highlights interpersonal skills necessary for building and maintaining relationships. Relationship skills encompass the emotional, cognitive, and social abilities that enable individuals to initiate, develop, and maintain healthy and rewarding interpersonal connections. Here are some examples:

Domain	Key Relationship Skills
Emotional Awareness	Understanding your own emotions and the emotions of others
Communication	Listening actively, speaking clearly, and expressing oneself honestly and kindly
Empathy	Seeing the world from another's perspective and responding with compassion
Conflict Resolution	Navigating disagreements constructively and respectfully
Trust-Building	Being dependable, consistent, and maintaining confidentiality
Boundary Setting	Knowing and respecting limits in oneself and others
Collaboration	Cooperating, sharing responsibility, and valuing others' contributions
Support and Care	Offering encouragement, help, and emotional support in times of need

Offering training to develop these important skills could enhance the social climate. However, supportive cultures are necessary to make these skills truly useful. Individual change tends to fade in environments that lack support. If the emphasis is solely on personal skills, it is likely that the changes will not be sustainable. These skills hold value when they are integrated with changes at all levels, with the community, organization, and group.

Don't Let Myths and Misunderstandings Undermine Your Efforts

Throughout this book, I have addressed numerous common myths and misunderstandings about social climate attitudes and behaviors. There are several additional myths and misunderstandings related to the overall goal of creating healthy and productive social climates. These misconceptions can cause groups to overlook essential steps or depend on ineffective strategies.

Myth/Misunderstanding	Reality
Nothing will change unless top leaders take the lead.	While leadership support helps, culture is shaped at every level. Peers influence each other daily through their tone, actions, and norms. Middle managers, team leads, and even informal influencers can shift dynamics within a subculture.
A good social climate happens naturally if people are nice.	While kindness helps, a strong social climate requires intentional policies and practices that support inclusive decision-making, shared goals, mutual support, and open communication. It doesn't evolve by chance.

Myth/ Misunderstanding	Reality
If no one is complaining, the social climate must be fine.	Silence can signal disengagement or fear of speaking up. A good climate fosters openness, not just the absence of visible problems.
Social climate is a nice 'extra'; it's not essential.	The social climate serves as a fundamental condition for well-being, inclusion, resilience, innovation, and productivity.
One toxic person ruins everything, and there's nothing you can do.	While an individual can exert a strong negative influence, a supportive social climate can lessen that person's impact and help facilitate necessary changes.

Begin Your Journey Towards a Healthy and Productive Social Climate

Throughout my more than 40-plus years of assisting governments, businesses, and communities in addressing their pressing and often perplexing social issues, I have come to realize that a supportive social climate is crucial to success. Strengthening, not undermining, the social climate is a necessity. This powerful cultural lubricant can bring people together in ways that were previously unimaginable. With a supportive social climate, our biological need for each other is no longer seen as an obstacle to overcome, but rather a virtue to be celebrated. Negativity, suspicion, apathy, and alienation no longer undermine good ideas and follow-through.

Adversity often brings people together in support of a common cause. Still, you don't need to wait for a crisis in your household, workplace, or community to enjoy a healthy and productive social climate. Connect with your friends, family, and coworkers to strengthen the social environment within your groups. By using some of the social climate-boosting tools and strategies in this book, you can enhance the social climate right now.

References

Chapter 1: Discovering the Power of Social Climate in Our Lives

Allen, J. (1998). *Working Well: A Video for Creating Healthier and More Productive Work Climates*. Produced by Vermont Educational Television. Available from Healthyculture.com.

Allen, J. & Allen, R. F. (1990). A sense of community, a shared vision, and a positive culture: Core enabling factors in culture-based change. *Community Organization: Traditional Principles and Modern Applications*, Edited by Robert D. Patton and William B. Cissell 419.

Allen, R. F. & Allen, J. (1987). A sense of community, a shared vision, and a positive culture: Core enabling factors in culture-based health promotion efforts. *American Journal of Health Promotion, 1:3,* 4047.

Davis, S. (December 24, 2023). New Year's Resolutions Statistics 2024, *Forbes.*

Kotter, J. P. (1995). Leading change: Why transformation efforts fail. *Harvard Business Review,* 73(2), 59–67.

Little, A.D. (1991, January). Linking Quality to Corporate Strategy. *Prism, 1(1),* 1–8.

McKinsey & Company. (1994, September). TQM and Partnering: An Assessment of Two Major Change Strategies. *PM Network, 8(9),* 22–26.

At Harley-Davidson, Continuous Improvement is a Multi-Pronged Strategy published by the Manufacturing Leadership Council, December 2018 available at https://manufacturingleadershipcouncil.com/at-harley-davidson-continuous-improvement-is-a-multi-pronged-strategy-9230.

Chapter 2: Measuring the Social Climate of Your Subculture

Allen, J. & Allen, R. F. (1990). A sense of community, a shared vision, and a positive culture: Core enabling factors in culture-based change. In *Community Organization: Traditional Principles and Modern Applications*, Edited by Robert D. Patton and William B. Cissell 4-19.

Allen, R. F. & Allen, J. (1987). A sense of community, a shared vision, and a positive culture: Core enabling factors in culture-based health promotion efforts. *American Journal of Health Promotion*, 1:3, 40-47.

Part I: Strengthening the Sense of Community

Block, P. (2018). *Community: The structure of belonging* (2nd ed., revised and updated). Berrett-Koehler Publishers.

Junger, S. (2016). *Tribe: On homecoming and belonging.* Twelve, an imprint of Hachette Book Group.

McKnight, J., & Block, P. (2010). *The abundant community: Awakening the power of families and neighborhoods.* Berrett-Koehler Publishers.

McMillan, D. W., & Chavis, D. M. (1986). Sense of community: A definition and theory. *Journal of Community Psychology*, 14(1), 6–23.

Putnam, R. D. (2000). *Bowling alone: The collapse and revival of American community.* Simon & Schuster.

Part II: Creating a Shared Vision

McLain, D., & Pendell, R. (2023, June 13). *Why trust in leaders is faltering and how to gain it back.* Gallup. https://www.gallup.com/workplace/473738/why-trust-leaders-faltering-gain-back.aspx.

Collins, J. C., & Porras, J. I. (1994). *Built to last: Successful habits of visionary companies.* Harper Business.

Coyle, D. (2018). *The culture code: The secrets of highly successful groups.* Bantam Books.

Gallup. (2024). *How strengths and wellbeing work together to create thriving workplaces.* Retrieved from https://www.gallup.com/cliftonstrengths/en/653777/strengths-wellbeing-work-together-create-thriving-workplaces.aspx.

Senge, P. M., Smith, B., Kruschwitz, N., Laur, J., & Schley, S. (2008). *The necessary revolution: How individuals and organizations are working together to create a sustainable world.* Doubleday.

World Health Organization. (n.d.). *UHC service planning & models of care.* Retrieved from https://www.who.int/teams/integrated-health-services/clinical-services-and-systems/service-organizations-and-integration.

Part III: Fostering a Positive Outlook

Achor, S. (2010). *The happiness advantage: The seven principles of positive psychology that fuel success and performance at work.* Crown Business.

Kegan, R., & Lahey, L. L. (2016). *An everyone culture: Becoming a deliberately developmental organization.* Harvard Business Review Press.

Lewis, S. (2011). *Positive psychology at work: How positive leadership and appreciative inquiry create inspiring organizations.* Wiley-Blackwell.

Oakes, K. (2021). *Culture renovation: 18 leadership actions to build an unshakeable company.* McGraw-Hill Education.

Patterson, K., Grenny, J., McMillan, R., Switzler, A., & Gregory, E. (2021). *Crucial conversations: Tools for talking when stakes are high* (3rd ed.). McGraw-Hill.

Seligman, M. E. P. (1998). *Learned optimism: How to change your mind and your life.* Pocket Books.

Now Is the Time to Strengthen Our Social Climate

Brooks, D. (2023). *How to know a person: The art of seeing others deeply and being deeply seen.* Random House.

Cohen, D., & Prusak, L. (2001). *In good company: How social capital makes organizations work.* Harvard Business School Press.

Office of the Surgeon General. (2023). *Our epidemic of loneliness and isolation: The U.S. Surgeon General's advisory on the healing effects of social connection and community.* U.S. Department of Health and Human Services. https://www.hhs.gov/sites/default/files/surgeon-general-social-connection-advisory.pdf

Ornish, D. (1998). *Love & survival: The scientific basis for the healing power of intimacy.* HarperCollins.

Turkle, S. (2011). *Alone together: Why we expect more from technology and less from each other.* Basic Books.

www.ingramcontent.com/pod-product-compliance
Lightning Source LLC
Chambersburg PA
CBHW071846090426
42811CB00035B/2339/J